MANAGEMENT ACCOUNTANCY
FOR THE
COMPANY EXECUTIVE

MANAGEMENT ACCOUNTANCY FOR THE COMPANY EXECUTIVE

T M WALKER

Published by Kogan Page Ltd
in association with
the Chartered Institute of Management Accountants

|C| I |m|A|

Incorporated by Royal Charter
63 Portland Place
London W1N 4AB

First published in 1981 by the Institute of Cost
and Management Accountants.
Copyright © ICMA 1981

This edition first published in Great Britain in
1987 by Kogan Page Ltd, 120 Pentonville Road,
London N1 9JN, by arrangement with the Chartered
Institute of Management Accountants.

British Library Cataloguing in Publication Data

Walker, T.M.
  Management accountancy for the company
  executive.
  1. Managerial accounting
  I. Title
  658.1'511   HF5635

  ISBN 1-85091-353-6

Printed and bound in Great Britain by
Mackays of Chatham Ltd, Chatham, Kent

CONTENTS

ACKNOWLEDGEMENT

Some parts of this book were first published as articles in the journal of the Institute of Bankers in Scotland and are reproduced by kind permission of the Editor.

Chapter 1

GENERAL INTRODUCTION

The vital resources of a business, manpower, money, materials and machinery, have in recent years been joined by *management information,* in the provision of which the management accountant has an important part to play. This book is about the role of management accountancy, which should essentially be directed from Board level, and which centres on the provision of management information necessary to enable an organisation to achieve its objectives. The information provided should facilitate rapid movement in the direction laid down by the Board, and is consequently designed to promote *decision making.* To achieve this, the information must be timely, accurate and meaningful. "Accuracy" is rarely, if ever, sought nowadays in absolute terms: the degree of "accuracy" needed depends upon the purposes of information reports provided.

The reader should realise that personal domestic life provides many situations where management accounting techniques can be used to good effect in helping hard pressed individuals to deploy limited resources to optimum effect: household budgeting and cash flow forecasting, for example, are a ready means of practising management accounting techniques and understanding how one decision can affect the whole broad canvas of one's affairs. In understanding management accounting, there is no need to focus on companies with million pound destinies.

Reverting to a business environment, the provision of information can be very expensive. Consequently, before the management accountant can feel comfortable about committing time and effort, he should discuss his output with those who think it would be useful (his colleagues), and refer to a simple check-list with their help:

(i) **Cost justification**

A monetary evaluation of the benefits to be derived from the information requested has to be weighed against the additional costs incurred in setting up and operating the system which provides the information. Many benefits lack sharpness of definition, and difficulties can be experienced in evaluating them in monetary terms. However, management should be trained in measuring the implication of work well done in financial terms. For this reason, it is in the interests of the non-accounting managers to have knowledge of the financial yardsticks which are used in measuring their own performance.

1

(ii) **Degree, persistency and quality of demand**

The demand for more or improved information should be reasonably consistent, free from ambiguity and forward looking to meet future as well as present needs. Most user departments (those who receive information from the management accountant) are so concerned with their day to day problems that they are not able to take the long, careful look that is necessary to determine the underlying causes of these problems. Most departments will, therefore, request systems that solve short range and superficial problems. Users will state their requirements without thinking them through carefully. Each time that they give a little more thought to the system being developed, they will change their requirements. In this manner, a management accounting information system under development can change direction several times, with each change delaying the project and destroying some of the enthusiasm of the management accountant. The best approach, therefore, is that systems requirements are determined with the approval of both user and management accounting departments. To achieve best results, members of the management accounting function should be offered training in appreciating areas of the business such as stock control theory and practice, production control theory and practice, marketing and distribution.

To facilitate maximum teamwork, some companies appoint a manager to lead the user departments in defining their reporting requirements, and in specifying them to those actually creating the information reporting systems. This appointment accelerates the search for a comprehensive approach to the objectives to be achieved through implementation of any new system. The "user spokesman" may in such cases be free from line accounting duties, spending his time crossing and recrossing functional lines on organisational charts to achieve a broad picture of all the problems. He generally has an accounting background, but because of his role, he must quickly drop any alliance to a specific business function. He should try to ensure that not only are the correct decisions made in specifying new systems, but that these are correctly balanced in terms of teamwork, ie all those interested have a proper sense of having contributed towards the decision making. In this way, morale remains high throughout the organisation.

(iii) **Top management support**

The support of *general* management must be gained, whose responsibilities extend beyond functional boundaries. While requests for new or improved information may well originate from the head of a particular function, there must be a grasp of the implications of such requests to *other* areas of business activity, and this is best dealt with by general management who maintain a fertile association with representatives of all functions. Without this top management involvement, a management accountant can be pulled ever deeper into partisan cross-fire as each function fights to secure its own needs. In any event, top management realise more fully than functional management that good information reporting systems, tools of and not substitutes for management, will strengthen both the horizontal and vertical structure of their organisations by assisting management at lower levels to make accurate and timely decisions.

(iv) **Top management authorisation**
The commitment of manpower and money must be in harmony with an organisation's budget pattern. While small improvements to and developments of existing information systems can be sought by and provided to customer departments without top management's seal of approval, it is imprudent to indulge this trait, as the changes sought and supplied are bound to cost money. The best way to test top management's *support* is to place before them a draft budget for the potential cost of the new or improved information to be provided. If this is not done, the management accountant can become increasingly pre-occupied with a damage limiting operation to stop actual management accounting and associated costs from climbing too far in excess of budgeted costs. "If I'd known that this new information was going to cost *that* much, I'd never have agreed to it . . ." is not a pleasant assertion to hear *after* massive accounting cost variances have occurred.

(v) **Feasibility**
The basic data needed to generate information should be available subject to agreed timetables and accuracy tolerances. The standards to be satisfied by good management reports are demanding. They should properly consist of concise statements of fact, timely presented in an accurate and convenient form which will enable the users readily to perceive the significant factors and trends within their fields of responsibility. If meeting such rigorous specifications is not possible, the feasibility of proceeding at all may be put in question, unless a compromise can be reached. The essence of the problem is that managers anxious to obtain timely output reports are at the mercy of others who are

responsible for feeding data into the system, and who do not see the necessity for speed. In addition, the basic data upon which the reporting fabric is built may be unreliable, due perhaps to faulty coding or the need for guesswork in apportioning or attributing costs.

There are, however, frequent discoveries at the feasibility stage that information can still be useful with reduced accuracy tolerances and/or when produced later than originally intended. A whole range of possibilities for amendment should be reviewed during feasibility studies, based on the old saying:

"I have six honest serving men,
They taught me all I know.
Their names are Who and What and When,
and Why and Where and How."

For example, the question could be asked: "What method of providing information best combines economy with ease of conversion into timely, accurate and meaningful information?"

On the question of good basic data, the choice of data to be used is, of course, tempered by many factors, eg its reliability, availability, value in the short term and value in the long term. While the first three are vitally important, it is usually in the fourth that the future wellbeing of the organisation is vested. Helping to plan the contents of the computer data banks, for example, will be one of the most challenging and rewarding jobs undertaken by management in the eighties.

(vi) **Operational staffing**

The qualifications and training of required operational staff should be carefully assessed. *Individual* responsibility for specific facets of new procedures and systems is an essential ingredient if staff are to pay attention during training meetings. Five o'clock on a Friday afternoon is *not* the best time to hold such meetings, nor are rhetorical questions of the "Do you all understand?" variety ideally suited to winkling out doubts and misunderstandings. To a large extent, information systems can only be as good as operational staff will allow.

Conclusion

Each business manager has to ensure the availability and/or appropriate flow of some kind of business resource. As the production manager works towards a flow of good output of production, and the manager in charge of finance, who heads what is commonly known in the US as the "Treasury Department", needs to ensure good cash flow at the right time, to the correct utilisation points and at economic cost, so also the management accountant has to ensure good information flow, again at the right time and at an economic and justifiable cost.

Chapter 2

THE IMPORTANCE OF TURNOVER AND SALES POTENTIAL: SALES BUDGETING

Ill-advised selling achieved in deference to the need for turnover can spoil the market for the selling company concerned and its competitors. To achieve this unhappy end result when cash to finance business is very expensive, the selling company needs only to offer one of the following ill-advised incentives to a potential customer: credit terms which are too lengthy; excessive discount; too early a delivery date, or too high a level of post-sales service. The management accountant has to set off various conflicting factors to enable decisions to be reached in the drive for turnover. Some managers could argue that any reasonable level of post-sales service could never be "too high" if it succeeded in prising business away from competitors: against this, if a profit margin of say 5% is involved in a transaction and the cost to a company of borrowed funds to finance production and outstanding customer invoices is 20%, a comparatively short delay in settlement by the customer can mean that the supplier company may have transacted the business "for nothing".

As a consequence of the above factors, the greatest care must be exercised in preparing a company's sales budget (or short term sales plan). In a healthy trading situation, the sales function will set a fast pace involving growth and new challenges to managers of the other business functions such as production and distribution. Sales provide the "spearhead" budget, behind which other budgets slipstream. In such cases, the company's market for its products is the limiting factor which restricts the company from limitless growth and profitability: the company does not need to turn business away, for example through restrictions on production capacity, shortage of raw materials or difficult distribution channels. A major danger therefore lies in removing bottlenecks such as capacity restrictions, raw material shortages etc at considerable expense to avoid clamping the anchors on sales growth, only to find that the sales budget has been ill-conceived in the first place. The best method of avoiding this danger is to exercise as much care and skill as possible in sales budgeting.

The following factors need consideration:
(i) Whether sales targets should be set initially in monetary turnover terms, or expressed in quantities or volumes and then converted to a monetary evaluation. A decision on this aspect depends on whether there is a

recognised limitation on customers' spending power. Sometimes market research is necessary. For example, some might say that a pub customer is likely to have £1 in his pocket, and when that is spent, departure time has arrived. If a price rise takes place, he is still likely to have £1, so that *the volume* of sales may drop. Others might say that such a customer will have a pre-planned volume consumption in mind in any event, so he is going to pay the going rate for this volume and then leave. The dominant view in sales budgeting is volume-orientated (ie, the latter view). The "£1 in the pocket" argument does have some influence, but this tends to be fairly long term. Many price increases during a financial year, despite popular opinion, do not significantly depress volume expectancy. Longer term, however, available spending power should be acknowledged as a major influence, as should pressures on volumes caused by competing products, (eg, lager versus ale).

(ii)   The extent to which increasing *market share* should be an objective. An increase in market share is often the first measure of worth in a highly competitive market, with each competitor pursuing marginal business in a market of known dimensions: therefore growth equals success. On the other hand, size in itself is not necessarily supreme in market place "muscle". The ability to service and maintain supplies to an existing range of outlets is vital in terms of long term investment and short term profitability.

(iii)   A careful definition of the company's income base. If sales budgeting is carried out early enough, opportunities are provided for considering the widening or contracting of the company's sales-generating activities. A traditional sales base can sometimes be extended with a little thought (eg, the BBC extending into BBC Publications). Again, the possibility of undertaking repairs and servicing can be relevant, or the acceptance of sub-contracting work to utilise spare capacity. In some circumstances, a company could hire out computer time and/or systems expertise. This whole aspect centres on the questions "Exactly what kind of business are we in?" and "Just what is it that we are trying to achieve?" These questions are frequently asked within a corporate planning framework, but they can also provide stimulation and interest during the annual budgeting process *if the company gives itself enough time.*

    The prosperity of a company selling a single product or service is tied to the wellbeing and corporate strategies of customers within a single or limited range of industries. There are risks from obsolescence, competition, failure of raw material supplies, lack of flexibility in capacity usage, nervousness among sources of finance, and from labour turnover resulting in loss of expertise.

(iv)   The influence of external factors, such as changes in the rate of VAT or changes in duty on say spirits or cigarettes. *Some* customers will continue to spend the same £1 after a VAT increase, with the unfortunate supplier retaining less of the £1 than previously. The extent to which this may happen can sometimes be determined through using a blend of market research and practical experience.

(v)   Timing of demand. Clearly the question of timing the sales demand across the budget period must be addressed for the sake of production scheduling and cash flow. There can soon be a "chicken and egg" situation, in that miscalculation on timing of sales can cause stock-outs of raw materials, sub-assemblies, components or finished goods, which in turn result in lost sales. In due course no-one is too clear whether a general company malaise has been caused by poor sales budgeting, stock control or production scheduling.

(vi)   The reliability of company resources, culminating in a confidence in the company's capacity to produce. A plan which seriously risks overstretching production capacity is usually caused by ignorance of what that capacity is. The consequences of a breakdown in resources include missed customer delivery deadlines, extended lead-times which damage chances of new or repeat orders, higher scrap levels caused by excessive pressures, and escalating costs through having to employ expensive temporary labour or accede to overtime or second-shift working. Measurement of production capacity is discussed more fully in the next chapter.

In general, the removal of a bottleneck which is inhibiting company growth, eg the purchase of new machinery or new lorries to ensure that market demand for the company's products is met, must be carried out in sympathy with longer term corporate plans, to prevent the company being stranded after a few months with excess capacity. Production and selling could lock horns on the former's failure to achieve output to satisfy sales demand in full, but the purchase of new machinery, or the employment of new full-time operators could cause embarrassment and financial problems later if the extra production capability was purchased merely to meet a short-term peak in demand.

(vii) Timing of product availability. This aspect is related to (vi), and concerns for example the conversion of pilot products which are up to standards and marketable to a mass-produced equivalent. Firstly, the company must come to terms with whether production engineering is really available at economic cost. Can the product *really* be mass-produced to the required quality specifications? Secondly, if the company is confident about the above outcome, *when* can goods be promised to customers? Sales budgets depend therefore upon careful pre-determination of the timing of events: total sales potential can readily be boosted or damaged if significant peaks and troughs in demand which could be out of step with finished goods availability are not winkled out in advance.

(viii) The significance of packaging and container types. The quality of sales forecasts of customer demand by, for example, packet size can make or break a company's performance against budget. Many managers do not relish the role of soothsayer and reader of entrails, but the company should insist upon earnest discussions about the prospects for individual products by container and/or package type. Eventually, it may emerge that this exercise is restricted merely to a pooling of ignorance: in such cases, outside market research may be the answer. Some companies classify products so that a standard product sold in various packages is developed into a product range. In any event, planning decisions are needed in good time before the beginning of the budget period to enable appropriate managers to arrange for supplies of containers and packaging materials. Careful monitoring is needed after container decisions have been taken to ensure that they are available on schedule.

(ix) Company policy on producing for stock or only to satsify particular orders. Many companies nowadays can no longer afford to produce goods on speculation. The cost of tying up cash in stocks in the hope of possible future recompense when overdrafts are so expensive, needs to be weighed up against the possibilities of lost sales if goods are not readily available. In competitive markets, lost sales may mean *more* than lost profits: the goods themselves may need to be written off with a consequent failure to recover costs incurred in production. Aggressive advertising can turn the market around in a particular company's favour, but this costs money, so that a company which has a ready supply of finance can thus inflict serious damage upon less fortunate competitors.

(x) Company policy on risks. A credit controller can be very useful in helping to achieve a corporate sales ambition with minimum bad debts. Risks of delayed payment however are highly significant, in particular in the field of export sales. A credit controller can prevent the erosion of profits through delayed payment. He will generally try to reduce exposure by shortening the company's credit base, eg by reducing the overall number of days' outstanding sales. He provides expertise in identifying and measuring risks, caused for example by shortage of exchange in importing countries, beaurocratic delays or poor and faulty documentation. Many credit control departments vet all financial conditions in export contracts. They also read the financial press for news items which have possible effects on risk. For example, a severe drought could damage a country's basic crop and cause a lack of earning power of hard currencies. This in turn would lead to hold-ups in the release of UK or other relevant currencies from that country in settlement of UK accounts.

In short, a sales budget can never be risk free, but management should be aware of the degree to which this budget is risk laden. The annual budgeting process provides an ideal time to review a company's ability to ferret out risks and opportunities. The company should ensure during the budgeting process that it has the capacity to negotiate good credit terms which make trading worthwhile.

(xi) Company policy on budgeting "from the grass-roots up" or from "top management down". Some companies, as a matter of immutable policy, issue growth targets for an ensuing year: "Budget for a 10% increase in sales: go to it". Others base company-wide targets on reports and opinions of lower levels of management who transmit information about the future as seen from the "sharp end" of the business. Clearly, these two approaches produce differing end results. A sales budget which is optimistic, however, has also to be realistic. Top management need to concern themselves with company image, the goodwill of shareholders and other sources of finance, etc and must achieve, somehow, sales budgets which make economic sense. Lower management, on the other hand, are much more aware of particularised conditions concerning environmental, social and population changes and their effects, eg a pub suddenly by-passed by a new ring road or motorway.

(xii) The effects of inflation. Management must face up to the prospects of customer resistance and the growth of substitute products during inflationary conditions. Every company is liable to be affected by inflation, so that a key objective lies in being *less* affected than the competition. Some companies make it their business to have substitute products to

9

offer, refusing merely to spend time recoiling from the effects of their imposition by others. Another target could be to attempt to contain selling price increases somewhere below general rates of inflation as evidenced by, for example, the Retail Price Index. At all costs, management should have a team policy for dealing with inflation. This involves, for example, early warnings from buyers of raw materials that disturbing price increases are in the pipeline, and signals from the personnel department about wage rate increases. Customers have somehow to be encouraged to swallow such inflated costs which are passed on firstly in quotations and price lists, and secondly in invoices. So the selling function needs as much prior notice as possible.

The damaging effects of inflation can be felt after a time-lag. For example, a manufacturer could succeed in offloading his goods to a retailer, but at *this* point customer resistance could stiffen to an unexpected degree. The consequences for the manufacturer would include a determined if not a desperate attempt by the shopkeeper to take as much credit as possible, with a sharp cutback in future orders placed on the manufacturer and with substantial discounting a major contention.

Faulty forecasting by those further along the trading cycle should be considered as a distinct possibility by manufacturers at the time of budget preparation, and attempts made to anticipate and ward off detrimental effects.

(xiii) Pricing policies. Allied to the above concern, is the need to establish price-volume relationships, showing the effects on demand of a range of possible selling prices. Market pressures may overshadow a company's leverage in this area, with weaker companies having to acquiesce to the policies of market leaders. A company needs to find out its own strength, firstly in influencing the general market's selling prices, and secondly, if *not* a market leader, in surviving a probable rough ride, with its waggon hitched to a market leader's wheel. The risk of a price war lies over some industries like a blanket. Price wars ultimately result in a thinning out of suppliers in the field, and are consequently provoked by those who are confident of being among the survivors.

A knowledge of the relative contributions to fixed costs and profits of each product in a company's range is helpful in choosing which products to promote, and where market share must be held or where it can be eroded.

(xiv) Optimum timing for the preparation of the sales budget. If a company has say thirteen four-weekly periods in its financial year, it may well start to budget for its ensuing year's sales around period nine of the current year. To wait any later would prevent various managers operating under the banners of other functions which support sales (such as production, distribution and finance), from mobilising their resources in time to be effective by the beginning of the new financial year. Late budgeting frequently carries the penalty of having built-in inefficiencies within the plans. In a rapidly changing modern environment, an earlier start to formalisation of figures can only be tentative. In every period of the year, there should be a built-in facility for reviewing opportunities, dealing with threats and for reviewing plans where necessary.

The actual volumes and monetary evalutions which make up a sales budget depend on information such as the health of the company's order book, customer plans and shifts in customer credit worthiness, the strength of competition and field sales reports.

Conclusion

Sales ambitions should be set within the framework of a strategy; for example,
 (i) to increase turnover;
 (ii) to maintain turnover but enrich the mixture by raising the proportion of high performance products to poor performers, with contribution frequently being used as the basis for performance comparisons;
 (iii) to increase market share.

Management accounting reports are useful in monitoring in due course, the success or failure to operate within such strategies, and consequent financial implications.

Chapter 3

THE CAPACITY TO PRODUCE: PRODUCTION BUDGETING

A budget or short-term plan for production requires careful assessment of *capacity*, to ensure that a company is physically capable of producing what is intended. Capacity can be defined as a capability to achieve a level of effort, and should be measured either as·(1) a number of units of *input*, such as direct labour hours, machine hours or departmental operating hours, or (2) a level of output such as litres or tonnes. A company must first create capacity and measure its size before sense can be made of a production budget or short term plan, which involves planned *exploitation* of capacity. Thus, if a company has identified a capacity of 1000 departmental operating hours, it may, subject to later comments, prepare a production budget of 1000 such hours' *worth of output.*

If extra capacity to produce is needed, this will probably cost substantial sums of money, possibly involving capital outlays and additional operating fixed expenses. So in turn, great care is needed to ensure that the sales budget is carefully prepared, to safeguard the company against a demand for increased production capability which proves to be a tinselly illusion. Extra capacity can commit the company to its use for a number of years if it is to make economic sense. So we have a strong link between budgeting and corporate planning. The former should be in harmony with the latter.

Defining the production workload

A starting point for the production function is frequently a precise definition of their workload. This in itself is by no means sufficient in a multi-product situation, as all the products are likely to vary in content and the degree of resources and effort required for their completion. They can, however, be converted to a common measure, frequently direct production hours' worth of output. So, if product A is expected to take two hours to produce, one unit of product A is classed as "2 production hours". Time standards for each product are assessed. In a manual operation, a variety of products could be converted alternatively to the common measure "direct labour hours" with the expected hours to be directly charged to making each product by the operatives concerned, being agreed. Again, in a mechanised or automated operation, machine hours or departmental operating hours' of output could be regarded as the most appropriate measure.

The utilisation of capacity

Thereafter, the head of the production function has to know the *capacity* which he has available. Firstly, gross capacity should be assessed. If, for example, capacity is expressed as man-hours, *gross* capacity could be:
Number of direct operatives on the payroll per shift (say 20) × 3 shifts per day × 5 days per week : 300 man hours.

From this unrealistically high total, various deductions would be necessary as Table 1 shows:

Table 1

Line number			Man hours
1	Aggregate capacity: as above		300
2	*less* absenteeism and lateness (say 5% of line 1)		15
3	Net capacity hours paid for by company		285
4	*less* indirect time of direct operatives		
5	caused by: mechanical downtime	25	
6	training	30	
7	waiting for work	30	85
8	Total production time		200
9	Efficiency factor (or ratio) % (Note 1) say 120%		
10	Hours' worth of output		240
11	*less* hours' worth of scrapped production (say 10%) (Note 2)		24
12	Hours' worth of good output		216

Note 1. Because of a wages incentive scheme or a change in methods, or because performance measurement as regards the amount of output to be expected in one hour may be out of date, it is fairly common to adjust the company's expectation of what can be produced from line 8 to a new target at line 10. For example, if 200 hours appeared at line 8, but the quantity of output to be expected from one hour's effort had not been adjusted in performance standards to take account of improved training offered concurrently with an incentive scheme, a factor of say 120% could be applied at line 9, with a consequent 240 hours' worth of output at line 10.

Note 2. Inspection reports, etc could indicate a failure of certain units of output to meet the company's required quality and/or accuracy standards.

A table along the lines shown can be used as a planning and control document. Figures can be entered in the "hours" column as part of the production budgeting process prior to the budget period, with the production function's key objective of production output to be achieved, shown at line 12. The line 12 total must take account of closing stock requirements, as well as the need to supply the selling function, and targeted output can of course be reduced if there is opening stock available at the start of the period. Sometimes a company will start with the "bottom line" 12, and work back up the table: "here is what you need to produce; now organise yourselves, working your way back up the table . . ." When the "hours" column contains anticipated future performance, the detailed exposure of the assumptions made, for example at line 2, can put management on enquiry, so that insertions which cannot stand scrutiny by the management team, perhaps through being too optimistic or pessimistic, can be adjusted. Changes to one line to make targets more realistic have a "knock on" effect. When a major change has to be made to a particular line but management require line 12 to remain unchanged, it can be necessary to rethink line 1, perhaps by employing further operatives. In due course, actual performance can be set against the planned hours and hopefully remedial action can be taken to correct any "slippage", or, alternatively, arrangements made to underpin any favourable trends.

Efficient use of capacity

The *efficiency factor* can be a pivot for the whole operation. The company's measurement of how much the production team can "get through" within an hour of direct effort becomes a form of standard upon which departmental manning and payroll levels are based. Engineering estimates are frequently needed when machines are involved to convert suppliers' assertions on machine capability to realistic equivalents under the operating company's normal operating conditions. A table of the above kind requires a timescale. It needs to be established for a particular week, month or other accounting period. When there are peaks and troughs in demand which have repercussions on production scheduling, tables should be prepared for the necessary short intervals so that they can still be used to monitor actual results.

Anticipating capacity utilisation problems

The production function cannot expect to operate at a consistent, unchanging capacity level. Not only is a definition of capacity available essential, but also the ability to operate safety valves which have been identified and confirmed in advance during the budgeting process as likely to be available if needed. If the required production level is not being achieved, this could be the result of internal malaise within the production function, or the cause could be a rethink by the company about the "line 12 target". In any event, the head of production can consider:

(a) overtime;

(b) extended lead times (stretching deadlines for completion hopefully with the approval of management colleagues);

(c) sub-contracting;

(d) a raised efficiency level (at line 9);

(e) a change a quality/accuracy tolerances; both as an aid to speeding up production and to provide safer passage for product units from line 10 to line 12;

(f) increased capacity at line 1.

If the problem is minor, however, small adjustments at lines 5-7 could rectify matters.

The need for indirect time

The relationship between direct and indirect time should be planned, authorised and monitored. Indirect time bites into the total paid time at line 3 of the table. The line 3 total can be reduced on account of searches for the correct tools, waiting for the ideal machine to become available, and training to increase operator efficiency, both in achieving production throughput and in optimising setting up and dismantling operations. Consequently, an element of indirect time should not only be tolerated but is positively desirable. Effective use of indirect time can mean fewer direct hours available, but that each is utilised to better effect.

Reserving a proportion of capacity

In addition to the safety valves itemised above, there ought to be a "cushion" or "buffer" of time somewhere in the plan to help the company to: seize unexpected opportunities; grow at an unexpected rate; allow for changed product specifications.

If reference is made to Table 1, it can be seen that a production budget aiming at 216 hours' worth of good output is well within reach. If this budget level is approved, there is no facility whereby the production function can respond to an unforeseen opportunity or challenge, *all else being equal*, by doing *more* than achieving budgeted output. Consequently, many companies would add additional hours at line 1 of the table, so that if the need arose to produce extra hours' worth of output in addition to the specified 216, there would be a corresponding capability without alteration to agreed percentages and proportional weightings elsewhere on the table.

Monitoring product performance

A watching brief should be kept on each product manufactured, to:

(a)   identify preferences for scheduling, should the company be in a position to rank products when insufficient capacity is availabe to meet market demand in full;

(b)   ensure profitability;

(c)   identify where ground can be lost with a minimum of detrimental effects, ie through lost orders or through escalation of costs.

This is best achieved by calculating, both at budget time and during the budget period, the monetary contribution per standard minute of output of each product. Such a contribution would be derived by charging direct costs such as direct materials, direct labour and direct expenses and deducting this total from the selling price of a particular product to arrive at its contribution to overhead costs and profits. A variation on this exercise involves charging the above direct expenses plus a portion of variable production overheads to a product to derive, by deduction of *this* total from the sales price, a contribution to *fixed* overheads and profit. Variable production overheads are those which are incurred in manufacturing a product, and which would cease if the product were not manufactured.

The importance of operating conditions

A production budget table similar to that previously described should be built to operate under the envisaged normal operating conditions for the budget period in question. If actual operating conditions vary from the "normal" used for the built-in percentages established on the budget table, lateness, absenteeism, efficiency, wastage etc will all prove to be substantially different in practice from expectations. There should be adjustments to the plan if a proportion of the production effort is to be carried out during overtime or second and third shifts; conditions tend to be quite different then from those "from nine till five".

Accepting less than the optimum

Depending upon management's philosophy, varying degrees of inefficiency and undesirable elements can be admitted and built into a production plan, so that actual results in due course are measured against second rate targets. Clearly it is imprudent to indulge this trait. The human aspects of budgeting have attracted more literary coverage in recent times, and there is no doubt that a company's general performance can be influenced by whether employees regard the budgeting process as a chore, a personal threat, or a stimulating and rewarding challenge to improve and thus gain job satisfaction and more material personal rewards. While it is beyond the scope of this publication to indulge in psychology. Piet Han's short poem is worth repeating in this context:

Mind these three,
T T T.
Hear their chime
Things Take Time.

Timing

A rushed job of budgeting allows no time for effective "brainstorming" and the company should always allow management sufficient latitude. Hurried or skimped training of relevant staff leads to serious misconceptions and downright errors. As far as the company is concerned, these all become sharks in the water . . .

The effects of decision making

Top management frequently need to know comparative incremental turnover and costs caused by altering aggregate capacity levels. This need not involve only capital expenditure; the removal of other limiting factors can bring extra capacity within reach. Reference is being made here to substantial policy decisions such as the introduction of a second shift, the acceptance by management of the need for regular overtime working at premium rates, or the building of a factory extension. In such cases, the management accountant will define the options open and compare costs and contributions per product unit and/or per standard minute/hour of output for each option. This procedure is often referred to as budgeting for various "brackets". As soon as a decision is made materially altering capacity, the company enters a new bracket and contributions are re-assessed. Clearly, decisions are taken on simulated results. The greatest care is needed with simulations or models of this kind, as they represent pre-visions of results under operating conditions and at capacity levels under which management experience may be flimsy or non-existent. The lists of assumptions made in support of each business option's financial outcome must be comprehensive and fully communicated to all concerned.

Flexible budgetary control alters out of date targets set at originally envisaged activity levels, so that they remain realistic for actual activity levels. This technique of *simple* flexing is adequate only if originally planned and actual activities lie within the same "bracket". When activity skims (or lurches) into a fresh bracket, there can, of course, be an uplift of *fixed* costs, but reference is being made at this stage to changes in the unit *variable* cost (involving direct materials, direct labour and variable overheads).

Management should continually address the question of capacity adjustments and the consequences of such decisions, but the annual budgeting exercise provides an obvious rendezvous point on the calendar each year.

Capacity expressed in unit volume

As mentioned on page 12, some companies express capacity in units of output such as tonnes or gallons. Such an arrangement again involves an initial detailed set of sales forecasts for the ensuing budget period. The availability of production plants is studied and an attempt made to prepare a production budget to manufacture the forecast needs of the business to meet selling targets. Capacity would be talked of in terms of, say *tonnes of production*. Let us assume in this case a fully automated plant is in operation.

A *theoretical capacity* would be established, ie the maximum, name-plate capacity of the plant, fully utilised, and operating under good but realistic conditions. Theoretical capacity, however, is anchored by the fact that there is a bottleneck stage; it is the maximum throughput through an established, accepted bottleneck stage.

Assume theoretical capacity to be 1,000 tonnes.

Effective production capacity would usually be substantially lower than this figure, owing to the need to spend time rectifying work; or the need to scrap some tonnes of output, or because of the pattern of manufacture involving less than ideal setting up and dismantling times and procedures.

Assume this to be 700 tonnes.

In due course, a further gap is likely, between the 700 tonnes above, and *actual production*.

Assume this to be 500 tonnes.

Management will wish to take a number of important steps involving in essence a comparison of the site's effective production capacity and the theoretical capacity, and the examination of ways of bringing the two closer together. This exercise is, of course, vital when the site is production limited, ie cannot make enough tonnes to meet market demand. Methods of narrowing the gap would include planning longer run-lengths of manufacture, thus reducing the number of shutdowns for cleaning, or slight variations in the pattern of make which could lessen the risk of sub-standard product being produced. There could also be a programme of recruitment if management could identify a bottleneck which could be overcome by additional manpower.

An output of only 500 tonnes could be caused by having shorter run-lengths than envisaged for 700 tonnes. In some processes, cleaning of machinery between production runs is an exacting and lengthy process, eg in the manufacture of dyes, paints, plastics, etc to remove traces of left-over colouring from preceding work. The effective production capacity of 700 tonnes could be based on, say, 15 tonne run lengths, and actual capacity will drop if the company is obliged, to meet market and customer demand, to operate on, say, 10 tonne run lengths. Problems of diminished capacity can also arise in maintenance when several "unplanned" problems appear simultaneously. Planned maintenance can be carried out by or with the assistance of contract labour but "unplanned" emergencies will need to be handled speedily by the company's own staff.

Conclusion

Identification of capacity is needed to measure production capability. Failure to understand one's capacity leads to stretching of lead-times. Witness the joiner who says he will "make a start the week after next". This may stretch to six weeks if he doesn't know his capacity to produce. Such a problem may have wide and long repercussions to the tradesman concerned. There is a sensitive relationship between capacity and production.

The management accountant will assist his company in:

(a) optimising capacity at minimum cost;
(b) optimising capacity utilisation at minimum cost;
(c) using capacity efficiently;
(d) measuring the financial implications of changes in capacity.

It *can* be acceptable to acquiesce in a gradual diminution of capacity utilisation in the knowledge that efficiency is increasing. The question is one of blending comparative cost assessments with the maintenance of flexibility and readiness to seize opportunities. As a corollary, there is a danger in obtaining new capacity, that it will create a surplus at least in the short term, so that management drop their guard on efficiency. Surplus capacity *can* cover up inefficiency. If a company's efficiency is out of condition, a sudden need to exploit every iota of capacity can prompt a disappointingly turgid reaction.

In general, a knowledge of capacity is needed:

(a) for comparisons with targets, previous periods etc;
(b) to monitor costs per unit of capacity and the cost of unutilised capacity;
(c) to assess and compare output achievements per unit of capacity;
(d) to monitor productivity.

However, the key purpose must be to measure production capability.

Chapter 4

THE CONTROL OF COSTS

Flexible budgetary control

The basic vehicle for controlling costs is flexible budgetary control. At best, this technique enables management to:

(a)   take decisions which will exploit and accelerate beneficial purple patch deviations from plans in a controlled way so that they become routine, and

(b)   nail harmful deviations before they cover the business like a blanket.

At worst, it can involve a dreary annual chore.

The master budget

Business objectives in the shorter term frequently culminate in the preparation of a *master budget.* The form which a master budget usually takes is that of a balance sheet projected ahead for one year. Production, buying, sales and the other functional budgets are orchestrated in an effort to ensure a state of affairs on the final day of an accounting year which includes a considerably enhanced revenue reserves total as compared with that on day one (before tax and distributions, etc) or some other clear sign of growing health and well-being. Between the two dates are many thousands, if not millions of detailed business transactions. The *essence* of management accounting is to monitor events at this business transaction level so that results at total budget level are in line with plans. If enough individual transactions can be generated which concur with expectations, the result must be the fulfilment of budgets.

A harmonious relationship between a company's master budget, functional budgets, departmental budgets and routine transactions can flourish if situation reviews can be provided to the correct people at appropriate times.

Budgeting for and controlling costs

We have already assessed the importance of *sales turnover* and *capacity to produce.* Sales and production activities, however, generate costs before income is earned. In ensuing chapters, we shall assess the main cost elements, such as materials, labour and production overheads, distribution and selling costs.

Management accountants can help their colleagues to achieve master budgets by warning not only of deviations from plan, but on the materiality of those deviations. On a day-to-day basis, management can be advised of the financial implications of various options which could be exercised for bringing a company back on course. Revisions to plans are sometimes necessary and not only can the management accountant express these in financial terms, but he can also measure the peripheral effects in areas indirectly concerned. The management accountant can evaluate any chain reaction which takes place across the organisation from a business decision which ostensibly affects only one function.

A parallel can be drawn with a householder who, in attempting to prepare, say, a holiday budget, finds himself drawn into a complicated inter-relationship with his prospects of income and commitments to other expenditure being vital strands of what becomes a total "master" package. In fact, prudence would direct him towards building within his plan some reading of tea-leaves on his whole state of affairs, perhaps a year hence. What bank balance does he want (or need) to have? Will he require a (new) car? Any endowment assurance policies? Clearly he can, and some would argue should, prepare a simple domestic balance sheet, and not make isolated, fragmented decisions which ought not to be taken while wearing "blinkers". Quite simply, trading organisations are on all fours with householders on the merits of such planning. The master budget is the result.

Having said this, the "cost of costing" should be recognised. For example, the key elements of cost should form the focus for attention. Too often insignificant overhead costs (in relation to total costs) can take up a disproportionate percentage of management planning and investigative time.

Because of the high costs of financing trading activity, a master budget nowadays will usually involve a targeted balance sheet, profit and loss account and *cash flow forecast*. The objective of high profits must be constantly shadowed by the need to have acceptable liquidity.

Conclusion

A master budget which involves crystal ball gazing normally one year ahead should be compatible with a company's corporate plan which paints a similar scenario sometimes for five and sometimes for ten or more years ahead.

Readers should try to draw parallels with personal financial planning.

The key objective of profit forecasting has now been joined by estimating of liquidity. Timing of costs and income day by day throughout a budget period are now more important than ever before.

Chapter 5

RAW MATERIAL PURCHASING

Interdependence between purchasing and sales budgets

During inflationary conditions, there is a heavy interdependence between raw material purchasing budgets and sales budgets. The volume of sales of many products depends upon raw material prices, eg chocolate biscuit sales forecasts may be impossible until the price of cocoa is determined. Moreover, items such as cocoa would usually be purchased on forward contracts with suppliers, and buyers would be unable to be specific about raw material prices unless they knew the quantity to be purchased and whether it was covered by established forward contracts. So buyers need to say in the above circumstances "You tell us the amount of the sales budget, and we will know how much cocoa we need to buy beyond forward contracts and provide an estimate of its possible price . . ." but the sales force reply "You tell us the possible price of cocoa and we will then provide a sales budget . . ."

Consequently, the reliability of the raw material purchases budgets depends more than ever nowadays on the credibility of the sales budget: a practical step must be to draw the sales and buying functions close together in the task of preparing budgets based on a close consensus of opinion. The need for a budget committee headed by a senior executive such as the chairman or vice-chairman is greater than ever.

In addition, buying forward has become more advantageous to facilitate a greater degree of reliability of buying price forecasts. If there is a decline in the demand for a product, evidenced in sales budgets, the buying department may be able to give prices because they are covered by forward contracts.

Buyers should work closely with the sales function as well as with engineering, research and development, to determine whether there are substitute products which customers would prefer if their first choice is becoming too dear. Consequently, raw material purchases budgets could be prepared with more confidence if excess supplies could be utilised in the manufacture of alternative products or grades of products.

Analysis of finished products

Raw material budgets are frequently based on the analysis of finished products into raw material constituents; for example, an electrical engineering company might break down its product into:

	% *weighting*
iron castings	0.10
steel sheets	0.30
copper	0.15
other raw material and fuel	0.30
semi-finished goods and other manufactures	0.15
	100.00

Establishments such as the Henley Centre for Forecasting are able to provide carefully researched percentage changes of one year's costs against the previous year, under headings such as those above, so that a company using their services can, in fact, forecast the overall percentage increase in its raw material costs.

Raw material stock levels must, of course, be carefully monitored and physically checked, so that any "topping up" of existing stocks by means of further buying can be done with complete reliability. Thus there is a need for sound book-keeping and stock control procedures.

The effects of inflation

Inflation brings problems to suppliers of raw materials as well as to their customers. The trick is for a customer to anticipate these problems and how suppliers could pass on their effects. In some cases, the use of substitute raw materials could be considered in place of those previously accepted.

Without a standard costing system which ferrets out revision variances and leaves traditional price variances, a raw material buyer may be tempted to purchase inferior quality raw materials in the face of unexpected inflation, lest he be blamed for high price variances. The use of revision variances places responsibility for only the "controllable" portion of total price variances at the buyer's door. On the other hand, revision of standards as an alternative to revision variances, may frequently be ill-timed and need to be done again.

Another general problem is in deciding what raw material price variances can be passed on in due course to the purchasing company's customers within increased finished goods prices. A knowledge of likely customer resistance and what format it will take is essential.

General criteria in raw material purchasing budgets

There are several strands in the pattern of raw material purchasing budgets: these must take account of

(a) quantity;
(b) quality;
(c) cost;
(d) timing.

(a) Quantity

The company's stockholding policies need to be defined and understood. One school of thought advocates a smooth passage for all production work, in that there are virtually no threats of raw material stockouts. Another is prepared to risk stockouts for the sake of holding down what can be substantial financing and storage costs. A buyer aware of his company's aversion to stockouts is likely to add a "buffer" of stock to allow for possible misjudgements of demand from production. The extent of this may depend on previous experience. The calling off of small quantities "by inches" across the budget period increases costs considerably, but on the other hand, commitment to bulk buying means possible lack of manoeuvrability later on: the company may be forced to retain less successful products in its range until raw material stocks have been depleted to a level at which only a small balance has to be written off. When raw materials are scarce, security of supply may be of paramount importance.

Particular quantities must take into account the reliability of the sales budget; the buyer must try to have emergency sources "on tap" at economic cost.

(b) Quality

The company's buyer must liaise with management colleagues on the effects which various raw material qualities have on production yields, scrap levels and operator and machine speeds. The possibility of substitute products should again be explored. Threats to supplies of preferred qualities of raw materials must always be reported in good time to management so that possible customer reactions to "knock-on" changes to finished product quality can be assessed.

(c) Costs

Again, warnings of greatly increased costs must come forward quickly. While the company's management may approve inflated buying prices, the company's customers may *not*, when these are passed forward on sales invoices.

A key objective of the buying department is to secure the optimum price for the company's required quantity: very often, there is conflict in that the ideal price (after discount) is for a quantity just beyond the required order quantity "band".

(d) Timing

By good timing, the buying department can minimise the company's working capital investment and transmit the responsibility for financing and storing such stock to suppliers. Clearly "good timing" depends on co-operation between the buyer and the production scheduling department. Also there is the need to assess lead times between purchase ordering and receipt of supplies.

There is a complicated network of communications to avoid disruptions to production (which would cause disruptions to sales) and to ensure that the company has cash available when required to pay its suppliers. There can be an obvious buying economy which can tangibly save money, but what is good for costs can cause pain to those trying to achieve selling ambitions. Typical ostensible economies, apart from quality changes which could alter the finished product, could involve an upturn in *risks.* "If we wait we *may* be able to get the stuff cheaper . . ." or "Supplier X *thinks* he should be able to make enough for our needs at 80% of the present cost . . ."; these are assertions which sound alarm bells (or should do so). By the provision of differential costs, the management accountant can ensure that management do not succumb to lures which do not support the company's objectives.

Conclusion

The annual budgeting exercise provides an opportunity to review the organisation of the buying function, eg whether to have centralised or decentralised control. A decision on this issue needs to take account not only of costing aspects but also where in the company the knowledge of sources of supply lies: clearly if expertise and knowledge can be attested at local sites, it could be ill-advised to establish a central buying department. On the other hand, if the various segments of a conglomerate speak with one voice, they can carry much greater "clout" with impressionable suppliers on price and delivery negotiations.

Chapter 6

PREPARING A LABOUR BUDGET: THE CONTROL OF LABOUR COSTS

Initial establishment of the workload

No matter how complex a company's operations, or conversely, no matter how simple, the production to be achieved needs a sharply focused definition, which, as described earlier, may be a number of standard machine hours, or standard direct labour hours, or standard departmental operating hours. For example, if management required 10,000 loaves to be made in a bakery, this could be converted to 10 departmental hours' worth of output if it is estimated that 1,000 loaves will be produced in an hour. If there are, say, three operatives in the department, a conversion can take place to 30 direct labour hours. The production manager will need to ensure that 30 direct labour hours' worth of effort are available at the required time; sometimes this will mean paying for many additional hours if there is an indirect labour "supplement" in the department, caused through each direct operator having to charge paid time to idle time, training, general maintenance work, etc. In addition, direct operators such as the three referred to in this illustration could well require support in the department from indirect personnel who do not actually produce loaves: cleaners, maintenance men, setters, fitters etc, all paid for and for our purposes, all requiring identification in advance and inclusion within the appropriate labour budget.

In another organisation, making say 3 products X, Y and Z, engineering studies could reveal the following pattern [st mins = standard minutes]

	Product X	Product Y	Product Z
Machine 1	2 st mins	3 st mins	1 st min
	(req'd per unit		
Plus:	of product)		
Machine 2	6 st mins	9 st mins	3 st mins

There would also need to be a specification of direct labour content per standard minute produced, say:
Machine 1: 1 Grade A operator minute at 8p, plus 1 Grade B operator minute at 7p.
Machine 2: 2 Grade A minutes at 8p = 16p.

A production requirement of a specified quantity in product units of X, Y and Z would come forward initially from management and this could be converted to standard minutes to derive in turn the number of Grade A and Grade B operator minutes with which the department would require manning.

Measuring the required number of employees

Moving to a further example, a small company might win a contract to manufacture to a customer's order specification subject to a deadline on delivery (say one month). The job would of course be fully analysed for content as a preparatory towards quoting. Each cost element would be assessed in turn: departmental routing would be envisaged, and the machines to be used, etc. To give some idea of the way in which labour costs can escalate under time pressure, the company's labour budgeting for the month can be imagined as follows, with one standard hour representing the amount of output of production reasonably to be expected from 1 direct labour hour of output.

Job no. 1160:		**1,000 standard hours**
Add: indirect time (hours):		
waiting for tools	80	
waiting for work	60	
machine downtime	60	
training	70	
	—	270
		1,270
Efficiency factor 80%		
therefore add 25% × 1,000		250
		1,520
Estimated absenteeism is,		
say, 5% of labour payroll		
therefore add 5% of x (payroll)		80
(95% of x = 1,520)		
Total direct operator hours		1,600
Rate of direct to indirect operator		
hours estimated as 1 for 1		
therefore add for indirect operators		
(hours)		1,600

An assessment for Job no. 1160 of 1,000 standard hours would mean that engineers etc considered that it would require 1,000 hours of direct time applied to it to achieve completion using normal methods and in normal conditions. However, to ensure completion of Job 1160 on time, the company would need to budget for 1,600 hours of direct operator time and 1,600 hours of indirect employees' time, almost all of which would be paid time. Whether such a total labour cost could be passed on to a prospective customer in a quotation would depend on factors such as the competitiveness of the market. Every effort should be made to prevent poor performance from being built into both budgets and quotations: so labour budgets should be prepared in good time to facilitate positive reactions to impending problems.

Redeployment of direct operators

In labour budgeting, an ability to shed or redeploy employees can be built in on a pre-arranged basis, if capacity utilisation is expected to be volatile. A constant labour force at varying levels of production and service department output involves the hazard of having to spread a heavy burden of costs over a few production units during quieter times. Nowadays, companies which have the ability to re-deploy proportions of their payrolls to other *useful* work at such times, or to shed them temporarily often have a major advantage. When such flexibility is not possible, it is important to achieve correct manning levels right from the start.

Conclusion

The following checklist of factors to be taken into account when preparing a labour budget again illustrates the need for margins of safety in planning and carrying out operations:

(a) Identify tasks to be performed.
(b) Prepare standards of performance, eg per hour, analysed by employee grade etc. Tasks at (a) can then be converted to hours' equivalents.
(c) Recognise operating conditions in these standards, with different standards for each set of conditions, eg according to shift.
(d) If machine or departmental capacity is paramount, identify capacity available and the percentage utilisation planned and prepare a labour budget which provides the necessary manning levels. Management need to know the labour cost of idle capacity and to monitor trends.
(e) Estimate absenteeism and lateness. In due course, management will want to know whether unexpectedly high or low levels could have influenced production volume surges or declines. Absenteeism and lateness are best analysed by labour category, so that causes can be suggested.

(f)   Estimate machine downtime at (d), and its effect on labour requirement.
(g)   Estimate labour indirect time for items such as training, waiting for work, waiting for raw materials, etc. It is useful for management to identify the labour cost of paid, non-productive time and to measure trends.
(h)   Budget for labour turnover. Standards of performance at (b) are set with a certain labour turnover in mind, eg with, say, a team of four operatives containing two experienced employees, plus one with, say, a year's experience, and one who is a comparative newcomer.
(i)   Assess budgeted headcount, for productivity measurement in due course.
(j)   Phase the budget over time periods to meet demand for labour when required.

During operations, a basic objective for the management accountant is to report the cost of unplanned events, such as disruption to production. Labour budgets need to be set up with this reporting aim in mind. Another is to discover developing trends before they go too far: for example, idle time can mean lost production which can mean missed delivery deadlines. Consequently, labour budgeting can be fairly complex, including at least a wide selection from the following items of information:

(a)   total labour hours available;
(b)   attendance hours;
(c)   capacity hours to be utilised;
(d)   headcount;
(e)   percentage absenteeism;
(f)   percentage machine downtime;
(g)   production in standard hours;
(h)   direct labour cost per standard hour produced;
(i)   indirect labour cost per standard hour produced;
(j)   total labour cost per standard hour produced;
(k)   labour cost per departmental operating hour;
(l)   labour cost as a percentage of total cost;
(m)   value added per £ of labour cost;
(n)   value added per departmental operating hour.

In the smaller company, (k) and (l) could usefully be used at very low administrative cost; for example, (k) illustrates the importance of production level coupled with high productivity levels when much of the labour cost in a department is fixed. At (m) and (n), value added may be defined as sales less bought-in raw materials and components, or, alternatively, as sales less all bought-in materials, components and overhead services such as power costs. A company should use whichever variant suits its own purposes and circumstances.

Chapter 7

BUDGETING FOR PRODUCTION OVERHEAD

Relationship to production volumes

A start can be made by establishing demand levels placed on production. A company can then budget to satisfy the production function's appeals for the help it needs if production targets are to be met. The production overhead budget is justified on the general grounds that it supports the production budget itself; when the latter has been authorised, necessary overhead costs can also be authorised in budget format.

Segmentation

Production budgets are segmented so that the whole function of producing becomes manageable by specific persons. So also the need to incur production overhead can be established by individuals in charge of cost centres or departments. The total of production overhead is an accumulation of the foreseeable costs determined at cost centre or departmental level in view of anticipated activity levels.

Measuring cost sensitivity

There is a need at budget time to distinguish between fixed and variable production overhead, the latter being those which in total will rise and fall in sympathy with changes in total production levels. Without this "cost sensitivity analysis", sensible reactions to actual cost incurrence during actual activity is impossible. Careful monitoring of cost behaviour during periods of stoppage, or during nadirs in activity, can provide useful information on realistic splitting of overhead budgets into fixed and variable elements. Management accountants frequently discover that so-called variable costs actually remain as a financial drain during disruptions caused by strikes, failure of raw material deliveries, power cuts, etc. The actual red warning light frequently takes the form of a steep and (initially) inexplicable rise in the company's bank overdraft.

Indirect labour within overheads

As mentioned in the previous chapter, a substantial proportion of production overhead occurs as a result of employing "indirect labour". In some companies, the ratio of indirect to direct operators can be as high as one to one. Indirect operators are those who do not charge their time directly (via time sheets, etc) to specific jobs, products or processes manufactured for sale. Nevertheless, their remuneration is as much a part of the end-product cost as direct labour, but needs to be apportioned to product cost on some arbitrary basis, eg as part of a departmental overhead charging rate per hour.

Budgeting for indirect labour requires careful consideration of manning levels and standards of performance or efficiency. As always, there should be recognition of the split between fixed and variable costs. In this way, budgeted costs can be flexed so that actual costs at actual production activity levels can be compared with what those costs should have been at actual activity levels.

Indirect time of direct operators

Direct production operators, ie those who can be expected to charge a high percentage of their time directly to specific jobs, products or processes, are, of course, involved in indirect time. When waiting for work, under training, or otherwise "not producing", most accounting systems require them to switch accounting codes for the time involved from direct labour to indirect labour (which is a part of overhead). The proportion of paid time to be incurred by direct operators which will be charged to overhead needs to be anticipated as part of the production overhead budget.

Timing of demand

As with raw material and direct labour budgeting, *timing* of demand is important. In most organisations, there are peaks and troughs in production and selling activity levels, and the supply of overhead services to production needs to arrive at the appropriate time. Maintaining in constant readiness the facility to service peak activity levels regardless of actual activity levels involves costly built-in "cushions" or "slack" which become apparent when analysing overhead cost trends per unit of production. If an organisation is resigned to such a situation, the overhead budgets will contain this padding of finance expected to pour out to ensure adequate response to activity situations which are not expected to arise. In due course, adverse variances of actual costs over budget will not show on reports, because the budget has been so loaded in the first place.

The general emphasis on timing is not only to avoid disruption to production or any slowing down of throughput rates, but also to ensure that adequate cash resources are available when required. The implications of all budgets are fed into cash flow forecasts, so that arrangements with sources of finance such as banks can be made with poise rather than panic.

Activity changes and their effects on costs

Nowadays, those who have a real facility to increase or decrease total production overhead as a result of changes in production levels have a worthwhile commercial advantage. The possession or lack of such an advantage should come up for review at the time of budget preparation. Of course, almost total automation in some industrial and commercial areas, coupled with employment protection legislation, has ensured that severe under-utilisation of capacity does not bring about significant drops in total production overhead costs. The proponents of automation anticipated the reduction of the cost rate per unit of production *provided that the level of units produced remained high.*

Budgeting for production overhead also provides an opportunity to discuss the extent to which fixed costs will *remain* fixed while planned activity levels change. Many fixed costs, sooner or later, leave the relevant range of activity levels in which they stay static, and rise or fall sometimes rather dramatically. Calls for extra output can mean new machinery, methods, factory layout or work shifts with a consequent raising of the total fixed cost level. Less likely, but still possible, declines in activity can result in the shedding of certain fixed costs. In either case, good budgeting means that actual costs do not come as a complete surprise. One aim in anticipating changes to fixed costs is to trace the possible effects of authorised overhead budgets upon product costs and selling prices and ultimate customer response.

Providing for additional demands

Expected levels of production may be exceeded, and provision has to be made for the ready supply of overhead services in such an eventuality. A boiler house, for example, needs servicing, maintaining in readiness, manning, insuring, etc on a hope and a prayer that production departments will require a supply of power. Having boiler house capacity "on tap" costs money, yet many companies prefer to authorise and pay for the cost of that part of the capacity which is not required, so that it is available in the event of unforeseen circumstances. This approach applies to many services areas, eg holding and paying for an expanse of storage area, perhaps only half-used, in case there should be a change in company policy on stock-holding, a sudden shift in customer demand, a widening of the company's product range, or a decision to take in sub-contract work.

Conclusion

The policy of authorising overhead expenditure to service budgeted activity levels is frequently loosened somewhat, especially as regards fixed overhead, to the authorisation of overhead to service the most optimistic forecast of activity, and even beyond such giddy heights. Management may often be anxious that the tightening of belts to eliminate the costs between most optimistic and budgeted activity levels would involve surgery which would damage the organisation's facility for growth at a later date.

Chapter 8

BUDGETING FOR ADMINISTRATION, SELLING AND DISTRIBUTION COSTS

1. Administration

The problem in budgeting for, and subsequently controlling, administration costs, is that flexing of costs allowed in budgets to take account of changed workloads and/or changed conditions can be very difficult. This is because precise definitions of workloads are frequently lacking.

Some organisations fragment the total weight of an administration function into portions, attributing each portion to other functions where they are grafted on in supportive roles. For example, accountancy might then cease to operate under "Administration" but be divided up so that part served the sales function, part the production function (eg a works accounting department or factory costing department) and part the distribution function (eg a transport costing department). The same treatment could be meted out to large sections of the personnel function, previously classed en masse as belonging to "Administration". Part of the personnel effort could then be on behalf of "Industrial Relations" (Production function), "Factory Recruitment and Training" (Production function) and so on.

The advantages of this arrangement of segmentation are that small portions of cost, previously classed as "Administration", can be expressed as percentages of the total costs of running the new "parent" functions to which they have been ascribed, and their worth in terms of useful service output measured more critically and yet more reliably by the parent functions' senior management. Indeed, in many cases, the parent functions have tangible, measurable output, so that, for example, accounting effort in helping the sales function could be measured as, say, 5p for each product sold at £5. The sales director might be in a good position to assess whether 5p was a reasonable cost for which real benefit had been obtained. Works accounting cost could be assessed as, say, 20p for each standard hour produced. In cases of the above kind, actual and planned costs would be compared.

The above comments are an oversimplification, as many administration costs must be incurred irrespective of any production, distribution, selling or other tangible activity. They are incurred to support efforts to maintain the "embryo" existence of a continuing business into the foreseeable future. In such cases, costs may be authorised as a percentage of total costs, or as a

percentage of production costs, or, on occasion, as a percentage
costs. There is also a dependence upon measurement of historical trend
year 2 costs could be authorised as, say, 120% of year 1 costs. Such a
approach is clearly undesirable when circumstances and conditions are
constantly changing and/or when management fails to assess whether value
for money is being achieved.

2. Selling

Such costs are largely supportive of tangible activity: nevertheless, they
should, for budgeting and control purposes, be divided into fixed and variable
elements, the former being incurred to maintain a sales function regardless of
specific selling activity, and the latter changing in total in sympathy with selling
activity levels.

Selling cost budgets will take account of the following factors:

(a)   competitors' policies: aggressive advertising, for example, is frequently
      matched in due course, "blow for blow" by others in the field.

(b)   product mix: extra costs may be authorised if there is a dispropor-
      tionately high level of new product launches in a particular period.

(c)   sales turnover: some companies approve selling cost budgets as
      percentages of turnover. If sales rise, the level of costs allowed also rises.
      On the other hand, products in decline are deprived of funds. Success is
      therefore rewarded and promoted, and failure is penalised and frequently
      accelerated.

3. Distribution

In budgeting for and controlling distribution (or transport) costs, an
organisation usually inherits a situation on a transport fleet. Budgeting for costs
has its "anchor" in such a fleet and past experience in coping with its transport
operations. The imponderables relate to any growth factors, inflation, changes
in shift-working policies or in operating patterns involving changing frequencies
of overnight stops by drivers, etc.

In general, distribution cost budgets slipstream behind forecasts of
increasing or decreasing selling activity. The effects of these forecasts on
numbers of vehicles, personnel and operating miles must be measured. Many
costs can be identified as "provoked" by vehicles, eg standing charges such as
insurance and road fund licences; others relate to employees, such as wages,
National Insurance and superannuation contributions, and, again, petrol, oil
and tyre costs relate to number of vehicle miles.

Vehicle numbers require analysis by vehicle type. In general terms, larger
vehicles are more economic as they involve a minimum number of trips to

such as tonnage. Variable costs per mile travelled are
vehicles, but the extra costs, eg involved in achieving
rom a 20 ton lorry as compared with 10 miles per gallon
d not outweigh the benefits of making far fewer trips with
rt a particular volume.

of transport budgeting is frequently carried out at local
depot level nout the country. Local managers, however, are more
concerned with physical stewardship aspects, such as the number of vehicles,
miles to be run and people to be employed. Financial evaluation of local
operations may well be carried out in a headquarters office.

Rigid budgeting at local depot level can be ill advised in that depot
managers may feel too restricted and unable to seize initiatives. While it is
difficult to "flex" budgets for minor changes in circumstances, local managers
require encouragement to maintain numbers of vehicles and employees at
optimum levels period by period, rather than strictly according to predetermined budgets.

For detailed budgeting and control, each vehicle usually becomes a "cost
centre" and each planned journey may lead to a costing exercise which relates a
proportion of budgeted cost to the "sharp end" of distribution activity. Each
new journey requires an estimate of time involved; total time is made up of
loading, travelling, unloading, finding the next load and moving forward to the
next stop point or returning to base. The cost of a journey attributed through a
costing system may well depend on the number of hours taken (for direct costs
such as wages, insurance and licence), and on the number of miles driven (for
costs such as petrol).

At the time of budget preparation, total costs are usually related to
particular depots, vehicle types and vehicles: in addition, estimated costs per
hour, per mile and/or per unit carried (tonne, pallet etc) are useful so that
decisions can be made about particular vehicles, journey types and depot
sitings.

Chapter 9

PURPOSES AND ADVANTAGES OF BUDGETS AND BUDGETARY CONTROL

During the long, slow climb through the budget preparation process, some illusion of sparkle may be achieved if managers are aware of purposes and advantages. Much can and should be expected:

(a) The provision of targets
Absence of motivation can muddy the clear view of individual managers on the need to achieve improvements in company performance.

(b) Relating targets to individuals
Budgets are usually set to be compatible with organisational structure. Budgets and budgetary control therefore segment company objectives into manageable proportions.

(c) Forcing teamwork
There must be a blending of effort, and a "trade-off" of expensive and frequently scarce resources among colleagues.

(d) Sparking off "brainstorming" about improvements
This can be aided by good timing and by focussing attention upon each separate manageable portion of responsibility. Important ideas should not be sent off in the mail to Head Office; they should be discussed on site.

(e) Forcing excuses into the open
Budgeting for failure should not be condoned. Limitations on performance there must be, but for reasons which are aired, discussed and authenticated by the management team.

(f) Identification of limiting factors
The "Terminology of Management and Financial Accountancy" defines a "limiting factor" as: "the factor which, at a particular time, or over a period, will limit the activities of an undertaking . . ." (4.46).

A limiting factor is sometimes a resource which, through short supply, inhibits the overall growth and increased wellbeing of an organisation:

Examples would be raw materials or labour. At other times, the market for a company's output may act as a limiting factor, in that the company can produce as much as, and more than customers want. Few managers feel comfortable about condoning the former type of limiting factor. Inadequate raw material supplies, for example, could damage capacity utilisation potential and could cause a lack of competitiveness.

(g) Ranking of limiting factors

Clearly all limiting factors can be removed, but at a cost. A primary limiting factor is the first one to clamp the anchors on growth and wellbeing. A secondary limiting factor is one which would replace the primary limiting factor, were it to be removed. Most companies have a tertiary limiting factor, and beyond. During budgeting, the sensitive entrepreneurial antennae on which management depend will tell them the position down the list to which limiting factors can be bought out.

(h) Provision of stepping stones towards the achievement of longer term plans

Each budget period, normally a year, provides milestone control for a company determined to achieve longer term corporate objectives.

(i) Highlighting deficiencies

Good timing offers each manager in the team an opportunity to become sufficiently supportive of overall company objectives by removing obstructive deficiencies in his own areas of responsibility.

(j) Cost sensitivity analysis

Management are keen to know total costs and costs per unit at various possible activity levels. They must also be able to flex costs in due course into line with actual activity levels. Cost behaviour patterns therefore can and should be discussed.

(k) Challenge to habitual costs

Cost can be incurred because it is "in fashion" to spend money in such ways. Again, the predecessors of current management may have condoned such expense. The control aspects of budgeting act as a counter to such dubious justification.

(l) Identifying critical activities

Clearly no company has a "bottomless purse" and management can decide on priority activities and how scarce resources are to be allocated. They are also encouraged to identify what they are offering or wish to offer to customers and to review the company's range of objectives.

(m) Identifying difficulties before they arrive

Most budgets "stretch" those responsible and success depends on squaring up to various difficulties en route through the period. Methods of coping with difficulties such as machine breakdowns, absenteeism, potential supply failures, etc can be optimised if they are considered in advance.

(n) Promoting action

Budgets and budgetary control in the proper hands can remove lethargy and carelessness.

(o) Identifying timelags

The sales function might capture an order, only for it to be produced many months later, with the company committed to a selling price which through inflation becomes far from satisfactory. The timelag between acceptance of customer orders and commencement of production is critical.

Budget timetables

A budget preparation timetable is essential to ensure completion of the various stages from initiation of draft provisional budgets by functional heads and departments reporting to them to ultimate authorisation of the master budget at Board level. The work of preparing, discussing and approving budgets for a forthcoming year is usually set against a background of severe work pressure to achieve current year targets. Consequently, any activity which distracts management from immediate problems and their solutions can frequently be regarded as a nuisance to be postponed until the last minute (or beyond).

Among the reasons for bottlenecks in reaching the stage of final budget authorisation are:

(1) Delays in deciding on budget figures to give areas of doubt and un-certainty regarding the future a chance to clear. Certain managers will delay making decisions on budgets for a future period on the basis that the closer they move towards the period, the more reliable will be the figures used.

(2) Delays as above to try to eradicate major assumptions which are necessary and which lessen the reliability of the figures. At the draft stage, and even later, when "final drafts" are presented for approval, the weight

of assumptions made may be unacceptable, so that draft budgets are returned to initiators for further investigation.

(3) Changes in organisational structure and/or in the constitution of a company, whereby preceding years' timetables are no longer relevant. For example, a takeover may have taken place, or divisions within a company may have been made into separate autonomous companies which themselves have a lengthier or a more streamlined approach to budget preparation.

(4) Departments preparing budgets may call for supportive historical information which may take a considerable time to gather.

(5) In general, revisions need to be made by originators of budgets and discussed with colleagues.

(6) Discussions about the significance of potential limiting factors: for example, when a company's affairs were buoyant, its growth could be temporarily impaired by a restricted delivery lorry fleet. Lengthy discussions might then ensue to find a suitable way of surmounting this difficulty. Lack of a solution would halt completion of the sales and production budgets.

(7) Other day to day hazards can affect timetable completion, such as unexpected staff shortages and faulty estimation of the work involved.

Conclusion

Any attempt to prepare small, segmented budgets should lead to a chain reaction involving entire operations. The fact that budgets are split into pieces, eg by function and by department, is really only a device to make budgeting practicable having regard to employee organisational (and responsibility) arrangements.

Budgeting also challenges users to make distinctions between hard work and clever work. "There's no substitute for hard work" is a dangerous cliché which should receive a basilisk look during budgeting. It is hard work, for example, to push in a five inch nail with one's finger.

Chapter 10

THE USE OF COST CENTRES

The actual mechanics of control and the preparation of budgets depend upon organisation. Most business enterprises are divided into functions, and each function is split into cost centres. To achieve its objectives, each cost centre is provided with a mix of resources, such as specific individuals, machinery, floor space and a licence to spend certain money.

Measuring activity

In controlling costs, then, the essence is to have a set of cost centres and within each a suitable way of measuring output of goods or services. In this way, it may be possible to react sensibly not only to comparisons of actual costs against original budgeted costs, but also to comparisons of actual costs against amended (or revised) budgeted costs at what they *should* have been at actual activity levels. So, if a salary bill has risen by 50% against the originally envisaged budget for a particular cost centre, this may, in fact, be a source of satisfaction to the manager in charge if the level of activity of the department has risen by, say, 70%.

There may be difficulties. It can be a fundamental problem to establish a unit or measure of output when there are, say, many different thicknesses, sizes or weights within a range of units produced. When there is heterogeneous output within a cost centre, it might be necessary to monitor costs per hour or per machine, to watch trends. Costs could be analysed into elements in such cases, such as electrical power, repair costs and insurance, to help identify the particular causes of any trend.

Where there are differing qualities, widths, thicknesses etc of output from a particular cost centre, and output period by period is measured in too general a manner, such as "tonnes per period — departmental total", considerable confusion can arise. For example, in a drop-forge department, the following figures could emerge:

Week 9 output: 146 tonnes
Week 10 output: 114 tonnes

Week 9 could be classed as a very good volume level, and week 10 poor, yet week 9 could lead to a loss situation and week 10 to high profitability, for reasons including the following:

(a) week 9 could involve a very high raw material charge, caused by excessive wastage and/or high value raw materials.

(b) week 9 could have a high level of products within the tonnage mix which contributed very little to the recovery of fixed costs and to profits.

(c) week 10, with its low tonnage volume, could have a high level of by-products which the accounting system allowed as valuable "credits" in the departmental performance statement.

(d) some of the week 9 output could fail to pass finished goods' inspection.

(e) the week 10 output could involve a more difficult mix of products in terms of machining and labour time, and could, within the restraints of a limited period, be commendable both in capacity to carry fixed costs and in saleable value. A higher level of skill could also be involved in week 10, with a consequently higher evaluation.

(f) week 9 could contain second shift and/or overtime premiums on labour costs.

An improved "common measure of output" such as standard hours would help to clarify the issue of which week had been the more successful. The tonnages involved would be analysed into more detailed "products". Over-simplifying the outcome of such an analysis, it could be found that:

Week 9 contained 146 tonnes of product A = 1460 standard minutes
Week 10 contained 114 tonnes of product B = 2280 standard minutes.

The basis for this discovery would be that the department was entitled to take 10 minutes for each tonne of A, and 20 minutes for each tonne of B. A logical step would, of course, be to calculate the contribution (sales value — variable costs) per standard minute for each product. In the above case, if the contribution rate per standard minute of A and B were identical, Week 10 would be classed as by far the more successful week.

Direct and indirect charges

The budget for a particular cost centre comprises:

(i) direct expenditure which can be traced to that centre as the prime instigator, eg the salary of a foreman belonging to that cost centre (say cost centre A);

(ii) indirect expenditure incurred initially for cost centre A by some other cost centre, say B, and apportioned to A, after being charged first of all to B for monitoring and controlling the costs concerned against planned costs, eg the salaries of maintenance men who belong to a maintenance department but who do work for "customer" cost centre A.

Thus each business transaction involving costs to a company is charged directly to *some* cost centre for control against planned costs. Each cost centre may, however, re-direct some of the costs thus charged if they have been incurred in providing services or other support to other areas of the company.

Non-manufacturing activities

Although care has to be taken with cost centres such as the drop-forge department above, when a cost centre is manufacturing saleable output, activity increases are relatively easy to measure and define. Within *non*-manufacturing activities, specific, definitive output is less easy to quantify and cost increases consequently less easy to justify. To facilitate cost control in such areas as repairs and maintenance, distribution services, power supply and stores departments, measures of activity should still be discussed and identified, so that when actual costs are incurred, they can be measured against amended, planned costs in the light of actual activity. (In achieving this comparison of actual and "flexed" planned costs, the company concerned must recognise that many costs may be fixed by nature, ie unchanging in the face of activity changes). The choice of measures of activity for control purposes will be in harmony with budgeting procedures for such activities, as managers concerned will plan to have in a budget period the capacity to supply service up to agreed levels; for example:

		Typical measure used
(a)	Repairs and maintenance	man-hours
(b)	Distribution services	tonnage-handling capability
(c)	Power supplies	(i) kilowatts of electricity from the National Grid and/or
		(ii) gigajoules of heat content for steam from own power station
(d)	Stores, say for finished goods	total tonnage storage capacity, with each store being designated as being for one particular product or product group, to prevent confusion arising from different product groups occupying different cubic areas per tonne

Overspending by service departments

Senior management *may* clamp down on overspending against original budgeted levels even if they can be "justified" through extra activity. In some organisations it would be pointless for, say, an accounting department manager to try to justify over-runs on his original cost centre budget by, say, 50% on the grounds that 70% more service was produced by his staff. The reaction from top management might well be that they did not *want* 70% more service. Extra accounting reports would then have been prepared on an unauthorised basis, doubtless for a company unable to afford them. Businesses, like householders, need to look at each area as part of a broad canvas. The above company, over-spending on accounting services, could well be short of cash to the tune of the adverse variance elsewhere in their spending pattern.

In short, therefore, over-spending on services against original budgets should always be treated with suspicion until fullest enquiries have been made. Those enquiries involve not only supposed cost justification of the extra unbudgeted services, but also careful vetting against corporate policies as to the shape and size of the company, its products and its operating strategies.

Apportionment of service department costs

The next pages are concerned with equitable methods of making sure that service department costs which are initially directly controlled in their own service department cost centres, find their way to manufacturing cost centres, because it is only at these latter points that saleable production activity is to be found. Manufacturing (or production) cost centres are therefore the attachment points for any service costs which rightfully belong as part of the product costs of products passing through on their way to completion. Service department re-apportionments arriving in manufacturing costs centres are merged with other costs which have been directly charged to the latter but which cannot be directly charged to particular products, to form a "total overhead" amount which is spread over production passing through the department concerned by means of an *overhead recovery rate* or *overhead absorption rate*.

Example:

Epsilon Limited has prepared departmental overhead budgets to be controlled within service departments and manufacturing departments as follows:

Service departments	£
Property	60,000
Personnel	8,000
General factory administration	38,000
Storeroom	7,250
Canteen (deficit)	6,200

Manufacturing departments	
Machining	88,000
Assembly	104,000

Management has decided that the most sensible product costs and valuations of work-in-progress stocks are achieved by using departmental overhead rates in order to charge to work-in-progress all costs apart from direct wages and direct materials which have been incurred in bringing stock to its present condition and location. These overhead rates are developed after appropriate service department costs are re-apportioned to production departments. Suitable bases for re-apportionment are to be selected from the following:

Department	Direct labour hours	Number of employees	Sq feet of floor space occupied	Total labour hours	Number of requisitions on stores
Property	—	3	2,000	400	20
Personnel	—	4	2,000	500	5
General factory admin	—	8	8,000	1,000	5
Store room	—	4	14,000	800	—
Canteen	—	8	12,000	1,000	40
Machining	10,000	40	40,000	6,000	400
Assembly	25,000	80	50,000	14,000	100

Required

Using a worksheet, re-apportion service department costs by the step method, and develop overhead rates per direct labour hour for machining and assembly.

Suggested answer

	Property	Personnel	General factory admin	Store room	Canteen	Machining	Assembly
1. Property @ £60,000/126,000 per sq ft	60,000	8,000	38,000	7,250	6,200	88,000	104,000
(47p rounded)	£60,000	976	3,808	6,664	5,712	19,040	23,800
		8,976					
2. Personnel £8,976/140 per employee		8,976	512	256	512	2,568	5,128
(£64.11 rounded)			42,320				

	General factory admin	Store room	Canteen	Machining	Assembly
3. General factory administration $\frac{£42,320}{21,800}$ per labour hour (£1.94 rounded)	42,320	1,552	1,940	11,640	27,188
		15,722			
4. Store room $\frac{£15,722}{540}$ per requisition (£29.11 rounded)			1,164	11,640	2,918
			15,528		
5. Canteen (deficit) $\frac{£15,528}{120}$ per employee (£129.4 rounded)				5,176	10,352
				£138,064	£173,386
Direct labour hours				10,000	25,000
Overhead rate per direct labour hour				£13.81 (rounded)	£6.94

Notes

(a)   The above detailed calculations are rounded. For example, the effect of rounding on the property cost centre has all been placed in the personnel column within the figure of £976.

(b)   Service department cost centres should be closed out in descending order of importance in offering service to the *other* service departments: for example, everyone needs a roof over his head and so the property cost centre has been cleared first. Then, every department has employees, so personnel has been cleared next, and so on. While the above principle regarding sequence is immutable, there is clearly, in practice, considerable subjectivity in selecting precise sequences in particular circumstances.

(c)   The top line figures for machining and assembly (£88,000 and £104,000) represent costs which have been charged directly to those departments but which could not be attributed directly to specific jobs, products or processes. They, therefore, *exclude* raw materials and labour which have been coded directly to jobs, products or processes via stores requisition slips and timesheets respectively.

(d)   The top line figures for service departments represent costs of running those departments which have been charged directly for control purposes, via basic documents such as suppliers' invoices, timesheets, stores requisitions, etc.

(e)   The "step method" of apportionment of service department costs involves recognition of the service which each service department offers to other service departments. For example, total personnel department costs are shared out, not only to manufacturing departments using that department's services, but also to any service departments whose accounts have not been closed further up the page, and who use personnel department services. Under the step method, when a department has been closed out and its costs re-apportioned, eg property (£60,000 on the top line), it is *not re-opened* to receive charges back into its account from other service departments.

(f)   Eventually, all of the costs along the top line have been moved into the two manufacturing cost centres: £311,450 is involved. The split between machining and assembly must be achieved as fairly as possible so that the costs collected in each are equitably charged to the two separate production outputs.

(g)   Throughout the re-apportionment process, the question asked in closing an account is "what factor provoked that department's cost?" For example, personnel department expense was assessed as having been caused by employing people, and it was decided that the greater the number of people employed within a "customer" department, the greater the share of personnel department costs would be charged thereto. Again, property costs were regarded as sensitive to floor area, so that the greater the square footage in other departments, the greater the charge made from the property department.

(h)   Any product, process or job passing through the machining department will receive a charge of £13.81 for each direct labour hour charged to it, to cover overheads. (In addition, the job will be charged with the cost of direct labour per timesheets, etc and direct materials per stores requisitions, etc.) Any product, etc passing through the assembly department will receive a charge of £6.94 per direct labour hour charged.

(i)   The company's objective in such cases is to generate enough chargeable business in the form of direct labour hours to "soak up" £138,064 of expected machining cost and £173,386 of expected assembly cost. If this objective is met, £(138,064 + 173,386) of costs of various kinds, which eventually attack the company's bank account balance, will be converted into part of the finished goods stockholdings evaluation, and, hopefully, recovered from customers through sales invoicing procedures. This mechanism for cost recovery would, of course, break down if insufficient direct labour hours were generated in practice and/or if actual costs incurred proved to be different from the given, expected figures. (The company is likely to "stick with" the rates of £13.81 and

£6.94 into the accounting period concerned, in the hope that activity and/or cost variances from plan will be smoothed out in due course.) Thus, if only 9,000 direct labour hours' worth of output passes through the machining department, and actual costs are, say, £145,000, the output will be evaluated at 9,000 × £13.81 = £124,290, so that there will be a shortfall between expenditure of £145,000 and stock evaluation of £20,710. In such circumstances, unless prices to customers were raised and/or other costs cut back, a loss would result.

(j)   Some companies employ the "direct method" of re-apportioning service department costs. Each service department's directly controlled costs are charged directly to manufacturing departments only; services rendered to other service departments are ignored. In the above example, the aggregate to be recovered against direct labour hours' of output would still be £311,450, but because of the "leap-frogging" method of moving costs rapidly to the manufac-turing cost centres, the split between the machining and assembly departments would be slightly different.

(k)   When actual costs at service department level differ from planned levels, the managers in charge may appeal for an adjustment to the charging rates used (whether the method used be "step" or "direct"). For example, if actual property costs proved to be £70,000 on the top line of Epsilon's statement, the manager in charge could try to force up the rate of 47p per square foot to a higher figure to recover the excess of £10,000. Management practice differs as to whether this should be allowed, but in any event, it would only be acceptable after full discussion as to causes of "overspending" and possible remedial action. The aspect to stress here is that variances between actual and planned expense are placed firmly at the door of the manager responsible for direct control of these expenses. In the case of the store room manager's cost centre reports at Epsilon, for example, £7,250 of expense would be headed "direct", and re-apportionments (£6,664, £256 and £1,552) as "indirect". He would be held accountable if actual direct costs deviated from the planned £7,250. If "customer" departments refused to accept increased charges from others supplying services, the deficits concerned would need to be written off to the company's profit and loss account as charges against profits for the period. Acquiescence on the part of "customer" managers to receive increased charges would often have a "knock-on" effect over several departments until eventually stock passing through manufacturing departments received not the originally envisaged charges, but increased charges per unit of output. Such uplifted stock evaluation would become part of the company's "cost of sales" in the profit and loss account when production was sold. The effect on the profit and loss account would be the same:

(a) Cost of sales based on unchanged service department
      re-apportionments   £x

     plus: written-off adverse variances from
      service departments   £y

     Total cost of sales per profit and loss account   £z

OR

(b) Cost of sales based on revised service
      department re-apportionments   £z

     plus: written-off adverse variances   NIL

     Total cost of sales per profit and loss account   £z

Conclusion

The preparation of cost centre reports comparing actual and budgeted results is one thing, the *interpretation* of these results is another. If interpretation is to be carried out successfully, deviations (or variances) must be categorised in ways which will optimise management decision making and action. Deviations from plan should be analysed between significant and trivial, temporary and permanent, seasonal and non-seasonal, and between those which are controllable by persons within the organisation and those which are not. Optimum rather than maximum reaction should be teased out of the above analysis. In some cases, no reaction at all might be the optimum level to provoke. Over-reaction can be based on management guesswork and "hunches" about deviations from plan; a good report will quantify and define such deviations and in many cases, take the heat out of a situation which might, for example, have precipitated an ill-conceived price increase or an inappropriate change of raw material supplier.

Deviations which have accumulated on a year to date basis can often be more significant than those for single months or four weekly periods. This is due partly to accuracy tolerance difficulties when trying to pre-schedule the exact dates of certain items of income or expense, and partly to fluctuations in operating conditions, levels of efficiency, scrapping, evaporation etc as well as activity level changes, which might be reflected in fairly dramatic short-term deviations, but which over longer periods, tend to lead to a reasonable equation of budgeted and actual results.

The optimum degree of detailed analysis is difficult to establish, and many mistakes can be made unless simulation tests are carried out at the systems design stage, or even earlier — at the feasibility stage — to test the value of proposed variance presentations to users. If a demanding, precise level of detail is called for, in due course various unjustified assumptions may need to be made on a rountine basis, to force transaction data into overdetailed categories. On the other hand, aggregate variances which in themselves fail to answer management queries lead to time consuming *ad hoc* enquiries, sometimes with the need for manual analysis of transaction records, to expose required levels of detail.

As a general rule, too much detail can divert the focus of concentration from key issues.

Chapter 11

STANDARD COSTING

Standard costing involves "the preparation of standard costs of products and services" (ICMA Terminology). Standard cost, in turn, is defined: "a predetermined cost calculated in relation to a prescribed set of working conditions, correlating technical specifications and scientific measurements of materials and labour to the prices and wage rates expected to apply during the period to which the standard cost is intended to relate, with an addition of an appropriate share of budgeted overhead. Its main purposes are to provide bases for control through variance accounting (2.312), for the valuation of stock and work in progress, and, in exceptional cases, for fixing selling prices".

There can be no doubt that the ultimate discipline in business is a comparison of overall total performance against budget for a period. But standard costing is invaluable in relating overall budgets to more minute circumstances, narrowing concentration to the elements which need attention at individual transaction level: the cost per unit of a raw material part, the throughput in units per hour of a particular machine, the oil consumption per hour of a particular boiler, and so on. Any degree of deviation from expectation or standard for each of the above items, triggers off a variance which may well have a bearing on the ultimate achievement of a budget. At this level, variances can be pinned down to specific causes and to specific people for attention*.

The significance of variances

Under standard costing, products, processes and jobs are given standard specifications of contents, representing the mix of resources and the costs of those resources which management *expects* will be required. Standard-building takes place in advance of actual operations, and consequently actual results obtained will tend to deviate from standards. However, a company using standard costing will put much effort into building sound standards, and will lay plans based on their achievement. So "variances" between standards and actual results, at business transaction level, build up over a period of time and reflect in total upon whether short term plans (or budgets) at departmental, functional and even company wide level are likely to be attained: and if not, why not?

Note: * *Paragraph quoted from my book "Understanding Management Accounting" (Gee & Co (Publishers) Ltd)*

Standards are useful in relating departmental objectives on performance, costs etc to individual transaction level. If enough business transactions are out of line with expectations, the company concerned will drift away from achievement of budgets.

Product specifications

To make sure that standards "bite" at operating level, output is analysed into its constituent elements. For example, if a company manufactures "Product X", its standard composition might appear as follows:

		Per unit of Product X £
Raw material item 1		3
Raw material item 2		4
Raw material item 3		7
Packaging		2
Direct labour		
Grade A	2 hours x £4	8
Grade B	1 hour x £3	3
Overheads		
£12 per direct labour hour (3)		36
Standard cost specification		£63

After determining a possible selling price of Product X, say £80, management can build expectations. They can begin to forecast the possible state of affairs of the company some distance along the calendar.

If analysis of actual results shows the cost of Product X to be, say, £67, standard costing, through explanatory variances with meaningful titles, with one variance for each deviation type, can focus the attention of individual managers on unplanned shortcomings and also strengths, so that, in later transactions falling into similar categories, weaknesses can be put right and strengths underpinned.

Standards as a means of control

Standard costing therefore breaks down deviations between short term plans and actual results into various segments, grouping like with like under variance account headings, to provide a clearer picture of why projected profit for a particular year may not be achieved, or may be exceeded. Meaningful titles are used for these variances, and these can be of value to particular managers.

A favourable "raw material usage variance", for example, would indicate that for the production output level achieved, less raw material had been used than was allowed in the standard specification. The production involved would have been deemed in advance to be worth, and capable of carrying, the *standard* raw material content, so if it had been produced more economically, say with £95 of materials used instead of the expected £100, the company would be proud possessors of stock worth £100 for an outlay of £95. The *plan* would expect a conversion of £100 of raw material stock into work-in-progress (material element) of £100, showing a balance of NIL. No profit would be expected. In practice, there would be enough work-in-progress to carry £100 of value, for a diminution of £95 in raw material stocks; the difference of £5 between the work-in-progress debit (charge) and the raw materials stock credit (reduction) would be a piece of good news.

Standard costing, and the "variances" which it produces, proliferate rather than stifle discussion.

Analysing variances by type

Most standard costing systems distinguish clearly between variances caused by deviations between expected and actual cost rates (eg tonne of materials, direct labour hour or kilowatt of electricity) and those caused by deviations in performance (eg number of units of production produced per hour versus standards, or the percentage of scrapped units versus standards). Each variance has its own possible root causes, which should be addressed by specific individuals. If a variance on, say, direct labour, between an actual cost of £14 and a standard of £11 (see Product X on earlier pages) were reported to a single manager, it would be unclear whether the unfavourable variance of £3 had been caused by paying for too many hours at the current (standard) rate, or by paying a wrong (non-standard) rate per hour for the standard number of hours, or by a mixture of both causes.

A wide range of variance types tend to be used by accountants because of the need to focus attention on many ways in which plans may have gone awry. On the other hand, too detailed a range of variances can force people to make assumptions about causes of variances just for the sake of completing the variance schedule on time. Ideally, variance reporting should be simulated in advance, to determine whether each variance, if reported "in real life" would actually be of help and likely to lead to decision making.

Standard Cost Variances

Understanding of standard costing and the use of variances can be greatly reinforced by examining one or two numerical examples.

Let us suppose that Beta Limited have budgeted to produce 500 units, but that they actually produce 550 units. For the sake of simplicity, we shall confine our thoughts to one element of cost, viz direct materials. In this instance, assume that the budgeted direct material cost at the original budgeted level of activity was £6,000, and that the actual direct material cost was £7,100.

It would be possible from the above information to calculate a direct material cost variance, as follows: £

(a) Actual direct material costs chargeable to costs of
      production in respect of actual production levels   7,100

(b) Standard direct material cost entitlement in view
      of actual production levels: actual production
      quantity × standard direct material cost per unit
      of production: $\frac{550 \text{ units} \times £6,000 \text{ original budgeted costs}}{500 \text{ original budget units}}$ 6,600

As the actual charge at (a) exceeds management's expectation for 550 units, the variance of £500 (£7,100-£6,600) is unfavourable. Notice how the expected or standard cost at (b) is "flexed" into line with actual production activity. It would cause unnecessary alarm to compare £7,100 or actual cost with the budgeted cost at a production level of 500 units (£6,000).

A direct material cost variance can be caused by paying non-standard prices for the raw materials concerned, or by using an unexpectedly high or low quantity of raw materials in production. Should the former situation be prevalent, a *direct material price variance* will arise, and in the latter case, there will be a *direct material usage variance.* Frequently both variances, totalling to the *direct material cost variance* need to be calculated as standard prices and usages can be very difficult to envisage accurately in advance.

In the above situation, a price variance could result from having to pay suppliers, say £12.50 for the standard raw material quantity allowance for each unit produced, against an expected or standard cost of £12. The price variance would then be: 550 × £(12.00 − 12.50) = £275 (unfavourable).

If the raw material quantity allowance per unit produced was agreed at, say, 300 lbs and actual usage totalled 310 lbs per unit, a usage variance could be calculated as follows:

	£
550 × 300 × standard rate per lb (4p)	6,600
less: actual usage × standard rate per lb (4p)	6,820
Usage variance: (£5 difference due to rounding)	220 (unfavourable)

Each standard costing variance should be reported to a specific manager for appraisal. If a variance is significant in size, likely to be repeated, and unlikely to be countered as a matter of course by compensating variances later in the year, remedial action may be necessary against unfavourable variances, such as raising selling prices of end products (if possible), introducing cheaper materials, eliminating or reducing raw material wastage levels or increasing the good yield of production from the input of raw materials by safeguarding finished products from breakage or damage. Equally likely, management may seek to find compensating variances in other areas of the business. The factors which cause certain unfavourable variances may have beneficial "knock-on" effects elsewhere which should be monitored by means of other variance reports: for example, an unfavourable raw material price variance may be caused by purchasing materials which are easier to handle and there could then be a favourable labour variance through processing more material per hour than expected.

It is customary for companies using a standard costing system to allow raw material, work-in-progress and finished goods stock to be recorded in their books at standard cost. So raw material, labour and overhead costs are then fed into cost of production (work-in-progress) at standard cost and when work is completed, the costs concerned are transferred from work-in-progress to finished goods stock at standard cost. Physical stock movements are of course reflected in the books of account, viz the nominal (or general) ledger, and it is possible for stockholdings to be reflected at standard cost in a company's balance sheet provided variances between actual cost and standard cost are insignificant. Sometimes favourable variances, which indicate the extent to which standard costs exceed actual costs, are held open as suspense accounts from one accounting period to the next, being absorbed into total stockholding figures so that the balance sheet evaluation of stock is not understated.

In the example which has been used above, management might well consider that the 550 units produced were not worth more than £6,600 in terms of raw material content. In such a case, a balance sheet extract might show:

	Original budgeted balance sheet (to reflect production of 500)	Budgeted balance sheet in view of actual production of 550 units	Actual balance sheet (550 units)
Source of funds	£	£	£
Revenue Reserves (deficit)	Nil	Nil	(500)
Bank Overdraft	6,000	6,600	7,100
Uses of funds			
Stock on hand (Raw material element within output achieved)	6,000	6,600	6,600

Such a presentation would be an admission that actual prices paid and quantities used were unnaturally extravagant, and that to encumber the ensuing year's management with opening stock containing £7,100 of raw material content would be unjust and could damage the performance of the company in the ensuing period as a result of a current malaise. Notice how, in the above balance sheet presentations, the £500 variance is being regarded as overspending, with no saleable output of finished goods on hand to show for it. Of the total expenditure of £7,100, only £6,600 is being regarded as sustainable as there are only 550 units on hand, each worth no more than £12 as regards raw materials.

Clearly, the above procedures are used for each element of cost which helps to make up the evaluation of finished goods produced. Direct labour, variable and fixed production overheads, and in some cases administration costs are given similar treatment, with variances between actual and standard costs being reported promptly so that adverse trends can be countered and favourable trends accentuated.

Conclusion

The more uncertain the future, the more standard costing can earn its keep. If plans are made which are based on achieving standards, a proliferation of variances, far from damaging the usefulness of standard costing, can provide fair warning of profit aspirations being well wide of the mark.

Standards must be set by individual managers, and certainly not by management accountants, except in very narrow spheres within the administrative functions where they may have some direct responsibility.

Chapter 12

MARGINAL COSTING

The technique of marginal costing involves segregating costs which rise and fall in sympathy with changes in activity levels (variable costs) from those which remain unaffected by such movements (fixed costs). Consequently, sensible monitoring of actual and budgeted expenditure (flexible budgetary control) and marginal costing have a common foundation in their dependence upon assessment of cost behavioural patterns.

Contribution and variable cost ratios

The word "contribution" features prominently in marginal costing. A particular product, process or job's contribution is the difference between its selling price and its marginal cost. If a customer were to pay £1 for an item sold by a retailer over a counter, and the contribution ratio involved were 40%, the shopkeeper would be able to put aside 40p from that £1 towards his fixed costs and hopefully towards achieving some profit. Conversely, if he knew that the variable cost ratio on the item was 60%, he would realise that 60p would need to be set aside to clear those costs arising directly because he traded in that particular unit of that product. So the sum of the contribution and variable cost ratios should be 100%.

Margin of safety

If the above shopkeeper's fixed costs for a period were £1,000, he would need to sell £1,000 ÷ 40p = £2,500 worth of that product in the period to reach what is termed the "break-even" point, the activity position at which he makes no profit whatsoever but, nevertheless, clears all his variable and fixed costs by means of his income. If his actual sales happened to be 3,000 units at £1, he would have a "margin of safety" between £3,000 and £2,500, ie £500 of his turnover would be beyond the break-even point and contributions from each £1 in this sector of his activity would be solely towards profit. The first £2,500 of his turnover would have soaked up fixed costs, with the final £500 not being needed for any such "absorption" task.

Ranking within a range of products

Many managers see the name of the game as enriching activity mixtures so that high contributor products are given preference at the expense of poor contributor products. Ranking of products is comparatively easy because the fixed costs of running a business are kept away from particular products. Attributing costs to products or jobs, etc is not plagued therefore by guesswork as to how to apportion fixed costs which cannot readily be earmarked, eg a work manager's salary.

Misleading results from spreading fixed costs

When an accounting system attributes *all* of the costs which have been incurred in bringing products to their present condition and location, the burden of the *fixed* proportion of those costs can force certain products into loss-making situations. However, to abandon such products would frequently involve the company in having to spread the same level of fixed costs over a smaller range of products, so that overall the company could become worse off without the so-called "poor" products. For example:

Product	A	B	C	Total
	£	£	£	£
Sales value	3,000	2,000	4,000	9,000
Cost of sales — variable	2,000	1,000	2,000	5,000
fixed	1,400	750	1,000	3,150
Total cost of sales	3,400	1,750	3,000	8,150
Profit/(loss)	(400)	250	1,000	850

Abandonment of Product A could well produce the following result:

Product	B	C	Total
Sales value	2,000	4,000	6,000
Cost of sales — variable	1,000	2,000	3,000
fixed (say)	1,350	1,800	3,150
Total cost of sales	2,350	3,800	6,150
Profit/(loss)	(350)	200	(150)

The loss of A's contribution of £1,000 to the constant fixed costs level of £3,150 would convert an overall profit of £850 into a loss of £150. The only counter to the above position would arise if the abandonment of Product A resulted in a genuine reduction in the total fixed costs of the company: but the reduction would need to be at least to the tune of £1,000. If the company's fixed costs included a charge for depreciation, elimination of products could certainly stop a continuing charge for depreciation of machines scrapped or no longer used. Accountants would point out that in essence depreciation charges would be accelerated rather than avoided: instead of the redundant machinery being written off in depreciation charges over a period of years, the period's accounts would receive the single shock of a full charge for the machinery's written down value.

Marginal costing as an aid to planning

Management can use marginal costing to simulate the future, and can project possible results across a range of options on, say, pricing policies without actually trading. For example, the shopkeeper could anticipate how many units he would need to sell to break even if his variable cost ratio on a £1 selling price rose to 80% and he was unable, because of customer resistance, to recover the cost increase through raising selling prices. (£1,000 ÷ 20p = £5,000 of sales would be required.) If, in the above circumstances, he could increase a £1 selling price by 10p, he would need to have a turnover of £1,000 + 27.27p per £1 of sales = £3,667. Determination of the margin of safety as a percentage of total turnover can provide an insight into how tenaciously cost increases must be combated if competition and customer resistance make sales price increases too risky.

Dangers in using marginal costing

The dangers in using marginal costing unquestioningly, include:

(1) Misjudging the behaviour of costs, so that the split made between fixed and variable costs is unreliable and leads to erroneous conclusions. In modern industry there is a danger in classifying any cost as "variable"; many costs thus described have not in fact declined with reducing activity levels. For example "direct labour" and "direct materials" are commonly regarded as variable: insofar as they are not *charged* to production if there is no production, they can be taken as variable; but frequently while production is not charged, the labour force concerned is still paid wages, which can be routed by courtesy of an accounting system to indirect labour and thence to overheads, where they wreak just as much havoc on a bank account as direct labour. In any event, when activity levels drop, skilled men are frequently redeployed into "indirect" activities at least for a while in the hope that business will revive. Again, drops in activity stop raw materials being charged into production, but they are still liable to arrive at and build up in stores, and need to be paid for.

(2) Misjudging the variable cost rate *per unit*. In crystal ball gazing about possible future activity levels, assumptions can frequently be made that when a variable cost rate per unit has been identified at, say, a company's *present* level of activity, this rate will appertain to all possible future levels: this despite the fact that the company may have had no recent experience

of operating at such levels. Variable cost rates per unit can vary, up and down, because of:

(i) changes in operating conditions, eg from a one shift to a double shift per day situation;

(ii) changes in the quality of resources available, once certain levels have been exceeded. For example, beyond a certain capacity utilisation stage, it might be necessary to employ trainees to perform work normally done by skilled operators. Again, optimum quality raw materials could run out after production exceeded a particular level, with the company being forced to use less than ideal materials which resulted in higher scrap levels or a slower pace of operations.

(iii) changes in the pattern of make. Switches from short production runs to long runs would normally cut the variable cost rate per unit, with larger numbers of units being produced across a typical working day.

(3) Acceptance by sales management of ill-advised sales orders, merely because they make a contribution to fixed costs. Attainment of contributions must be balanced against pursuance of worthwhile credit terms and conditions of sale (see page 5).

Best use of limited resources

Trading organisations usually hope that with the resources at their command, they will be able to satisfy customers' requirements and need not turn away business through any shortfall in, say, raw materials, machinery or labour. During extended periods of growth, such an attitude may have merit. The problem, however, lies dormant until the bottom drops out of a company's market. To maintain a growth trend, a company needs to be committed to purchasing additional resources to make increased activity possible. These resources include machinery, manpower and materials, and they tend to be wrapped in a package of fixed costs which remain long after growth has changed into decline. The adage "Never turn away good business" has been the undoing of many companies. Quite apart from labour and machinery, growth can involve bulk buying of materials and components which can require writing off if the market for the finished goods concerned turns sour. Nowadays the management accountant should consider not only "instant profitability" or "instant contribution" from particular trading carried out, but the financial implications, which may lie in the not too distant future, of a trading decline.

By the same token, automation brings economies of scale while operating levels remain high, but can be disastrous when trade declines, because such a high percentage of total costs are fixed and immutable.

With this backcloth in mind, many companies are hesitating before committing themselves to the prospect of more than one year of costs in the certain knowledge of one year's income. In consequence, they may resign themselves to factors which limit growth other than market demand. Some business is then turned away through lack of a full package of resources to handle any and every customer order which may arrive.

Typical scarcities include:
(a)   direct labour hours;
(b)   machine hours;
(c)   raw materials.

Management then strive to select those customer orders which offer the best contribution per unit of the resource which is in short supply.

For example, product A would initially be a clear winner in this table:

Product	A	B
Sales value (per unit)	£10	£15
Variable cost	8	14
Contribution per unit	£2	£1

But if A took four hours to produce, and B only one hour, with hours being scarce, the company would want to commit the production function to making B until the market demand for B was satisfied, and only then switch to making A until finally scarce hours were exhausted.

If, for example, only 24 hours were available in total, and market demand for A and B was for 20 units in each case, the company would capture a contribution of £1 for each hour committed to making B, but only 50p for each hour used up in making A.

Optimum choice

Product	A	B
Contribution per unit	£2	£1
Contribution per hour	50p	£1

Production schedule	Hours used	Contribution (£)
B : 20 units	20	20
A : 1 unit	4	2
Total contribution		22

In practice, limiting factors such as direct labour hours and machine hours tend to be compounded. For example, three factories within a group might be

61

chasing work orders being placed by group headquarters, with each factory having differing levels of machine and labour availability, and product types to be made requiring varying ratios of labour hours to machine hours. In such cases, the management accountant needs mathematical techniques such as linear equations to place the most appropriate work with each factory, minimising any wastage of resources.

Conclusion

In coming years organisations will be saddled with very high proportions of fixed costs as compared with previous decades unless they can adopt a "hire and fire" policy with *machines* used. Automation and other forms of mechanisation will bring a burden of fixed cost to which industry and commerce will be committed even in lean years, in much the same way as a householder might need to face mortgage, rates and annual car costs during a period of unemployment or part-time working.

From a heavy burden of fixed costs can come a lack of manoeuvrability. They tend to become part of the establishment, part of the penalty of holding capacity in a manned, secured and insured state of readiness. Thus management accountants need to advise not just on the basic split between fixed and variable costs, but on the degree of future commitment to continue with costs beyond the period when compensating income can be foreseen with certainty. They should also keep a watching brief on the proportion of *fixed costs to total costs;* as fixed costs, rise, management may be able to take advantage, in short term decision making, of a narrower "crawl space". Finally, the adaptability of the resources ranged under the heading of fixed costs needs to be maintained. Personnel, machinery, floor space etc should if at all possible be capable of change to recognise new challenges, threats and opportunities.

Having said this, the essence of marginal costing is careful examination of cost behaviour at differing levels of production, selling and distribution, etc. This task will remain vital both in monitoring actual costs against expectations, and in planning future courses of action, despite any increase of fixed costs in proportion to total costs.

Chapter 13

THE CONTROL OF WORKING CAPITAL

"Working capital" has been defined as "the capital available for conducting the day to day operations of a business; normally the excess of current assets over current liabilities".[1]

"Current assets" are "cash or other assets (eg stocks or short term investments) held for conversion into cash in the normal course of trading".[1]

"Current liabilities" are "liabilities which fall due for payment in a relatively short period, normally less than twelve months, eg creditors, bank overdrafts and provision for taxation and dividend claims".[1]

Liquidity in conflict with profitability

In a nutshell, this means that a "profitable" company, the sales of which substantially exceed the cost of those sales, *can* get itself in a tangle on liquidity. Most accountants can recollect classic examples. The managing director of a small company in oil distribution and road haulage, for example, discovered to his delight that his firm had made a profit of £15,000 for a particular financial year. On the strength of this, he went out and bought a new lorry costing this amount. A week later, he was shaken by a two-pronged attack by his accountant and his bank manager, who provided separate but identical news flashes that the company had plunged into a substantial overdraft. Considerable discussion was necessary to drop the scales from the managing director's eyes. The main points were:

(a) There had been growth of business towards the end of the year, and the new business had gone into debtors rather than cash.

(b) The elements of cost of trading were such that creditors could scarcely help at all to finance growth, and could therefore not ease pressures on the company's bank account. Most costs involved wages and fuel and even pre-payments for insurance and road fund licences. Repairs, spare parts etc had to be paid on the spot or even in advance.

(c) Stocks of oil had been paid for, damaging the bank balance, but the costs of closing stocks had not of course reached "cost of sales" in the company's profit and loss account; therefore profits were unscathed but cash was well down.

The above case illustrates the importance of grafting working capital control onto routine business planning and reporting.

The financing of current assets

Current assets need to be financed just as do fixed assets. A company has to pour money out before it can appeal to customers to mount a rescue operation by paying for goods supplied. During the delay period between delivery of raw materials to a supplier's factory and receipt of a customer's cheque for finished goods made from these materials, the supplying company is out of pocket, except to the extent that it, too, can lean on *its* suppliers by delaying payment for the raw materials.

By the same token, there can be a considerable timelag between paying wages for conversion of materials, components etc into finished goods and recovery of the cash involved from satisfied customers. Each element of cost (materials, labour and overheads of all kinds) has its own trading cycle which constitutes the delay period between cost incurrence by the manufacturer and recovery of that cost from customers.

Typically, a trading cycle for *raw materials* might be:

Average period in days

10	Raw materials lying in store awaiting call-off into production.
15	Period when raw materials in the factory being processed into finished goods.
25	Raw materials lying in store after production, as constituent part of finished goods.
<u>40</u>	Period in which raw materials element in finished goods is in customers' hands but not paid for.
90	Total number of days needed before initial raw material costs are converted back to cash on hand through recovery from customers.
<u>30</u>	Less: credit granted from suppliers of raw materials.
<u>60</u>	Length of trading cycle: financial help needed either from outside the business or from *other* parts of the business.

After 60 days, the company will continue to buy raw materials which need to be financed, but as money pours *out*, similar sums will pour *in* from customers settling their debts. If raw materials are needed *evenly* throughout the year, and there is a stable pattern of credit received from suppliers and credit given to customers, the company locked into the trading cycle shown above will be out of pocket and needing help from banks etc to the tune of: $\frac{60}{365} \times$ total annual raw material cost.

Clearly, anything the company can do to shorten the length of a trading cycle (in the above case, 60 days) the more financial and commercial benefits will accrue. Measures which might be taken to cut down on trading cycles include:

(a) More efficient production scheduling, so that production effort is directed to appropriate machines with minimum queuing.

(b) Better tooling, to optimise output for each direct hour utilised in production.

(c) Improved factory layout to speed work movement between processes or departments, and improved handling operations.

(d) Improved raw material, component, tooling and spare part stock control, to stop production from unnecessarily coming to a standstill as a result of "stockouts".

(e) Manufacturing whenever possible to customer orders rather than for stock.

(f) Invoicing customers on day of despatch rather than, say, collectively at each month-end.

(g) Improved credit control procedures as regards follow-up of outstanding debts.

The effect which an extensive trading cycle can have on a company's cash requirements can be illustrated graphically:

If Company A requires £60,000 of raw materials in year 1, and if production and sales take place evenly throughout the year, the need for cash from sources other than the trading operations concerned, (either from external sources such as banks, or from *other* trading operations) will depend upon the speed with which raw materials are used.

Suppose raw materials lie for
- one month in store
- two months in production (as part of work in progress)
- one month as part of finished goods
- two months in debtors

and they are subject to one month's credit from suppliers. There will be a subtantial need for finance, which will increase steadily until customers begin to pay sales invoices which include the company's raw material costs. The need for external financing from a source other than the trading operations concerned will rise steadily from February until a peak of £25,000 is reached in June. Thereafter outflows and inflows of cash in respect of raw materials will cancel each other out so that the need for cash remains indefinitely at £25,000. The broken line from the zero point shows the revised position of the outgoing payments line in the event of paying cash on delivery for supplies. If customers were to take an extra month's credit at any time after June, the company would immediately need to find an extra £5,000 from elsewhere to maintain incoming raw materials.

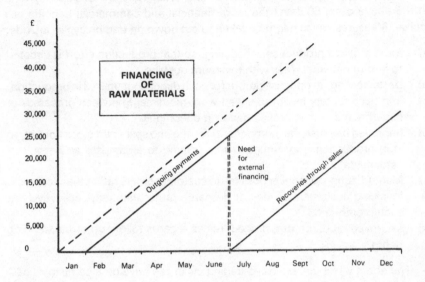

Stockout risks versus financing costs

Fine tuning is needed between, for example, cutting down on finished stocks made "on a hope and a prayer" that they might be sold, and missing opportunities for sales because finished stocks are not available to meet unusual surges in market demand. To a great extent, particular profit margins on goods sold have a bearing on whether a company should acquiesce to a policy of paying high overdraft interest to a bank to finance finished goods stocks for a number of months. Again, the ultimate profit margin on a sale to a customer who may take very protracted credit is paramount. If, for example, overdraft interest is, say, 20% and a customer buying goods on which the margin of profit is around 5% delays payment by four months, the transaction must be questionable. The supplier can come close, on occasions, to working hard for nothing.

Misleading ratios

Balance sheet ratios relating to working capital, which purport to offer evidence of the degree of efficiency brought to bear by a company in utilising, streamlining, and turning over working capital can be highly misleading. A balance sheet may ostensibly reveal excessive stockholdings, well above the company's immediate requirements. However:

"The more stock which management carries between stages in the manufacturing-distribution process, the less co-ordination is required to keep the process running smoothly. Contrariwise, if stocks are already being used efficiently they can be cut only at the expense of greater organisational effort — including greater scheduling effort to keep successive stages in balance, and greater expediting effort to work out of the difficulties which unforeseen disruptions at one point or another may cause in the whole process".[2]

A simple illustration of the above point could be used. If a factory had four consecutive processes through which production flowed, any unexpected machine breakdown at process three would cause a shutdown also at process four unless there was a "surplus" of stock lying between processes three and four, ie some slack which could be taken up to keep process four's wheels turning while the machinery was repaired.

Nevertheless, there are occasions when, by any yardstick, a company has stock which is genuinely excessive. After tests are carried out, no excuse can be found such as aiming for bulk buying benefits, or having to build stocks to meet seasonal peaks. The penalties depend on circumstances and the nature of the stock involved, but they can be severe:

(1) obsolescence, deterioration, risk of theft, damage and faulty storage.
(2) high costs of storage including rates and insurance, and high financing charges.
(3) loss through carelessness in handling and general usage. If production staff know that the storekeeper is holding large quantities of materials or parts, they will realise that, should they experiment in unauthorised ways with handling or working, or offer unscheduled involvement to trainees, or otherwise damage materials through lowered efficiency, there will be plenty of additional supplies.
(4) inflexibility of production: companies can become "locked in" to the production of certain products which they would normally abandon. Cessation of production would mean massive write-off of ingredients/parts, so the company concerned delays switching to more attractive products until such stocks are run down.

Holding stocks at depressed levels

The holding of *insufficient* stocks certainly dimishes a company's working capital base, so that costly financial aid from outside the company or from elsewhere within the organisation is cut back. However such savings must be weighed against:

(1)   the threat of production bottlenecks, which tie up working capital. As mentioned earlier, financing of the business through an overdraft is often based on estimation of the timespan through which a company will need to be financed until its customers "refund" the expenses of manufacture. If work-in-progress comes to a halt on the shop floor through waiting for missing parts which should have been held in stock, then the overdraft is likely to swell as costs continue to rise and the company's ability to recover costs from customers is delayed. The financing of new production, supposed to emanate from customers, has instead to be supplied by bankers.

(2)   vulnerability to risk of breakdown in supplies; if a company is living on a hand to mouth basis, there is total dependence on the timeous arrival of regular small deliveries from suppliers. Any breakdown in supplies can cause full scale stoppages. Countering such eventualities when they arise involves searching elsewhere for emergency supplies, but these may be of a different quality or texture which may cause handling or working difficulties.

(3)   vulnerability to high scrap levels; if excess stocks are not held, unnaturally high scrap levels may mean that customer orders are unfulfilled: the production foreman returning to the materials store for extra materials may be turned away. The inspector failing certain finished items at the last minute may unwittingly cause problems when there are no replacements for the finished goods rejected, and the company has to make up the lost quantity "from scratch".

The control of overtime

A manufacturing environment in which there are prospects of missing completion deadlines can lead to a proliferation of *overtime*. Operations which involve substantial premiums on basic wages certainly help to move work-in-progress towards completion at a faster rate across the calendar, but it must be remembered that the overtime premiums paid become embedded in the evaluation of work-in-progress and finished goods stock and in themselves put pressure on the finances of the company concerned.

If ways can be found to eliminate or reduce the deflections, bottlenecks, downtime, etc which arise during the basic working day, overtime should diminish. Steps which could be taken include:

(1)   the reduction of the amount of time needed for the re-working of spoiled products, by means of improved training, better tooling and generally improved motivation (including increased responsibility, where appropriate).

(2) the improvement of production scheduling and of the handling of materials and work-in-progress.

(3) re-scheduling of training if possible, so that it does not conflict with high activity periods or interfere with deadlines.

(4) aiming for a greater output from each direct hour's worth of effort. Such an improvement is often promoted through a productivity agreement or incentive scheme.

(5) reduction of absenteeism.

(6) redeployment of a higher proportion of operatives to directly chargeable work, and away from service departments. This can be regarded either as a stop-gap measure or can be organised on a more permanent basis, depending on circumstances.

(7) adding employees to the payroll. This will ensure a greater supply of labour during normal hours at normal rates of pay. Great care must be exercised: (a) to consider the *full* cost of such employees including pension payments, supervision and insurance costs and canteen subsidies against the *full* cost of overtime, including overtime premium payments, extra supervision, and heating and lighting; (b) to ensure that the need for extra labour is more than transitory.

(8) increasing machine capacity; overtime may well be caused by queuing for scarce machinery and equipment which is in demand beyond the close of the normal day.

Control of debtors

Another "suspect" ratio is that showing the relationship of debtors to sales, ie which broadcasts the speed with which customers pay their accounts. This ratio is sometimes specified as a "number of days' outstanding sales". For example, if a company's annual sales are £365,000 and the debtors total £20,000 at the close of the year in question, the number of days' outstanding sales is:

$$\frac{365,000}{365} \text{ divided into } £20,000 = 20$$

This purports to explain that, on average, a customer takes 20 days to pay his account: meanwhile, the cost of the goods involved is being laid out by the supplying company. Any attempt to prepare a trend over the years can be seriously distorted because:

(1) growth of new business towards the end of a year can inflate the level of outstanding debtors, giving the number of days' outstanding sales the appearance of being sluggish.

(2)   the debtors' total can be distorted at any time by a single dubious and overdue account, while the speed of debt settlement in general is actually improving.

(3)   the company's customer mix may be changing over the trend review period. For example, the company may have entered export markets or may merely have changed the proportions of export and home sales, with credit terms for export sales being vastly different to those for home sales. Again, a company could be changing its emphasis from wholesale customers to retail customers, with a consequent "distortion" to the length of credit being granted.

(4)   the company may be deliberately extending improved credit terms to customers to bolster order books and damage weaker competitors. In such cases, an extension of the number of days' outstanding sales can be *good* news, although a casual balance sheet reader, unaware of background details, would probably assume that it was bad news.

Credit control

A credit control department is frequently employed in larger organisations to maintain a careful interest in the level of customer debt. Its key objectives are:

(a)   to have the highest possible level of debt for the shortest possible time.
(b)   the achievement of corporate sales ambition with minimum bad debts.
(c)   the prevention of the erosion of profits through delayed payment.
(d)   reduction in corporate exposure through shortening of the credit base.

Such a department must be careful not to make minimum bad debts the *primary* aim: maximum profit should be allotted top place.

The routine work of the credit control department includes:

(1)   forecasting and monitoring shortages of exchange in countries importing the company's goods or services.
(2)   helping to make finance available, eg for trade expansion.
(3)   classification of accounts for risk, and the approval of credit based on product profitability as related to that risk. In general, the greater the profit, the greater the risk which may be taken.
(4)   assessment of collateral security and its acceptance in appropriate cases.

Members of the credit control department frequently study the financial press for news items which have a bearing on the risks of supplying particular classes of customers. As risks increase, the management accountant is called upon to produce statements of the contributions to fixed costs and profits resulting from taking those risks.

The control of cash

If a company is prospering, stocks of all kinds and debtors can hopefully all be converted into cash and bank balances. When that happens, good cash management is a valuable attribute. It is possible by means of skilled cash management policies to survive on a smaller amount of working capital than was previously considered possible.

Plans can be made to ensure that proper use is made of surplus funds, and negotiations with a bank or other organisation can be carried out well in advance of the need to receive incoming financial support. For example, some medium term sources of finance require six months' notice. Approaching cash shortages are identified thereby enabling management to raise additional funds of the right type and amount. Within the framework of a cash flow forecasting system, a company can compare actual with budgeted results and identify variances. In the light of the variances revealed by the comparison, the company can take remedial action, or if this is impracticable, revise the cash forecast.

Ideally, a *cash flow forecast* should:

(1)   highlight peaks and troughs in incoming and outgoing cash flow. For example, a monthly comparison of actual and planned cash flow could easily disguise problems within the month. On the other hand, a daily comparison would involve daily forecasting which would be bound to be inaccurate and throw up daily variances which could cause unnecessary alarm or jubilation.

(2)   project cash flow as far ahead as is possible without having to make nullifying assumptions. Many companies prepare "rolling" forecasts: at each month-end a new month is added and an historical month is dropped off. On any forecast report, there could be, say, 3 historical months and three future months. The next ensuing month might be detailed by week with the next two months after that showing totals only.

(3)   help to identify the best pattern of mix between overnight money, and short and medium term finance.

(4)   segment forecast and actual results to take account of organisational structure and individual responsibilities.

(5)   blend with other reports, such as profitability and contribution statements.

(6)   show any borrowing limits.

(7)   point up trends, but remove distortions to these by, for example, showing exceptional items separately.

(8)   identify potential large negative cash flows, which might, for example, prompt management to set aside impending capital expenditure.

71

Conclusion

The most important objectives in this area can be summarised as (a) the speeding up of inward cash flows and (b) the slowing up of outward cash flows. Clearly, as has been mentioned in the preceding text, arrangements can be made within the company concerned, with sources of finance, and with customers to ensure that these objectives are met. To maintain liquidity at minimum cost requires expertise to which the managers of *all* functions should contribute. The major benefit of good working capital management and control is perhaps the reduction of *risks*. Even the identification of the range of assumptions which have had to be made in trying to forecast working capital movements brings benefits to all facets of an organisation's operations.

1   "Terminology of Management and Financial Accountancy", (Institute of Cost and Management Accountants).
2   Harvard Business Review.

Chapter 14

THE CONTROL OF CAPITAL EXPENDITURE

There is a sequence for budget preparation and the capital expenditure (capex) budget is within that sequence. A capex budget for one year sets out to bridge the gap between where an organisation wishes to be in one year and where it *will* be if no capital expenditure proposals are implemented. It is in a sense a servicing budget — making other budget fulfilments possible such as production and distribution.

Categorisation of capital expenditure into, say, cost saving, replacement, expansion and hygiene/safety etc may bring in its wake sub-budgets for each category. These sub-budgets exemplify a company's specific strategies. The capex budget may be governed by a limit imposed through capital rationing, so that in times of scarce finance any category for which there is a high element of risk may be set aside.

Again, the capex budget may be based on a funds allocation so that the best projects brought forward for consideration are automatically selected provided they meet the finance charges involved and/or comply with some other criterion on profitability. The total budget may, however, be split and apportioned on the basis of a percentage to each segment of the organisation, so that the best projects within each segment may be selected.

Contents of a request form

A major role of management in the area of capital expenditure is to assess degrees of risk. Those who submit capital expenditure proposal forms for approval should remember that they must enable this role to be fulfilled.

The contents of a request form should include the following:

1. The category of investment

Items in the ''replacement'' category would involve trying to maintain existing facilities allowing neither decline nor expansion. There would be no change in the production capacity available, nor in products manufactured. ''Cost reduction'' project would emanate from the need to produce the same products at the same levels of activity but to do so more cheaply. (Frequently a measure of success is a reduced variable cost per unit.) ''Development'' would involve the introduction of new products. ''Expansion'' would bring about an increased output of existing products, and ''Hygiene and Safety'' would frequently be provoked by government or local authority regulations.

Each category of project has its own risk level, according to the industry concerned. Management's responsibility includes taking a view on the prospects for the particular trading operations of an organisation, especially when they extend over a range of industries. Proposal forms are addressed to those who have authority to approve the expenditure concerned. Addressees find categorisation in the above manner useful in helping them to make decisions as to the acceptability of projects. For example, when capital rationing exists, development projects must be regarded with great care. If £1 million were to be committed to a development project, there might also be a need to authorise, say, £2 million for other projects which were intended merely to maintain production of the company's basic traditional products: customer relationships would depend upon such products during future development phases, as in the past. This £2 million would include the costs of replacing worn out machinery, and cost reduction schemes aimed at making production of existing products more economic and competitive. £2 million would be an estimate, based on budgeting procedures. If actual cash requirements exceeded £2 million, there would be an immediate call for more funds, but, in cases where capital rationing existed, such extra funds would probably not be available (having been committed to development). The production wheels on main products could then grind to a halt for lack of capital, the main causes being faulty budgeting and lack of a "buffer" of cash; key customers could then suffer major reductions in service provided.

Clear categorisation of projects would also facilitate competition for "development" or "expansion" funds among the various segments of a group, in particular where capital rationing existed.

Requests for funds within certain categories could be identified as cutting across company strategy or policy — eg (a) for the expansion of bread baking capacity at a bakery location within a group fully intending to sever its connection with bakeries at an early, opportune date, or (b) for a "cost reduction" siting of a warehouse at a low population density site when company strategy for ensuing years involved siting production and warehousing at the centre of high population areas such as London, Liverpool and Glasgow. Each categorisation would attract differing degrees of risk: cost reduction might be risky if it fell foul of trade unions; expansion might be risky if competitors were likely to act more quickly than the company to satisfy increasing market demand; development might be risky if it meant manufacturing a product exposed to sharp changes in public tastes, eg skateboards, or a board game involving a television personality whose series had an indeterminate life.

The following table shows how each category of capital expenditure attracts its own particular *risks*. For the purposes of this illustration, the categories used are: (1) Replacement; (2) Cost Reduction; (3) Development; (4) Expansion; (5) Hygiene and Safety. Brief explanations of these categories appear after the table. The ticks are intended to suggest significantly important risks which apply to particular categories.

Description of Risk Item:	Replacement	Cost Reduction	Development	Expansion	Hygiene & Safety
1. Range of assumptions	✔	✔	✔	✔	
2. Obsolescence	✔				
3. Missed opportunities	✔				
4. On-line timing			✔	✔	
5. Conjecture about rejection	✔	✔	✔	✔	
6. 'Knock-on' effects					✔
7. Labour relations		✔			
8. May depend upon high-volume output		✔			
9. Changes in public taste			✔		
10. Additional working capital			✔	✔	
11. Lack of management experience			✔	✔	
12. Sources of finance may have misgivings			✔	✔	
13. 'Hidden' costs					✔

Commentary

Item 1 — In accepting a project in *any* category, assumptions must be made about the future, e.g. as regards competitor action, raw material availability, rates of inflation, economic trends, etc. However the range of assumptions which must be made varies in scope and in significance according to category: a wide range of assumptions frequently applies to all categories with the possible exception of Hygiene & Safety.

Item 2 — Simply to replace like with like is to risk being overtaken by technological advance.

Item 3 — Replacement can commit a company to continuation of the status quo perhaps for several years. There are frequently opportunities and risks in the environment in which a company operates, which would militate against continuation of old methods, etc.

Item 4 — If a company intends to develop or expand, it can be sure that competitors are considering similar courses of action. The successful outcome of projects in such categories can therefore depend upon winning a race with competitors to bring new premises and/or plant "on-line" at the earliest opportunity, to capture the market which is being pursued.

Item 5 — Those who propose projects frequently make assertions regarding possible outcomes if their projects are turned down. Proponents will know in many cases that these assertions cannot be proved or disproved and may become over-confident or careless in preparing the groundwork detail to support their projects.

Item 6 — Benefits to one department in a factory, or one factory in a group, can lead to proliferation of similar requests in other departments/factories.

Item 7 — Cost reduction *can* involve reduction of a company's labour force.

Item 8 — Automation is frequently promoted as a means of reducing the cost of manufacture per unit; however this advantage may only occur if production levels remain very high. When production levels are depressed, an automated plant can prove very expensive.

Item 9 — Development frequently requires a very long lead-time between authorisation of the project concerned and eventual start-up of production. During this delay period projected market-demand may, and frequently does, decline.

Item 10 — To the capital cost of development and expansion projects must be added considerable monetary commitments to support increased working capital requirements. Some categories of capital expenditure require heavy supporting working capital expenditure, while others require comparatively little.

Item 11 — Development and expansion projects place new responsibilities upon management who may as yet be untested in coping with related problems. A manager with a good "track record" in a stable environment may not succeed when new stresses emerge.

Item 12 — Outside sources of finance have their own views on risk, and these vary according to the categories of expenditure which a particular company may be promoting. A constant flow of external monetary support cannot be expected for every category of expenditure.

Item 13 — Some safety equipment affects operator speeds and therefore output rates per hour; for example, safety guards on machinery. Operating cost per hour must then be spread over fewer production units.

2. Description of project

This should be brief and reasonably free from technical jargon. An example of a project description supporting a cost reduction project might be: "The installation of an air-conditioning plant type xxx in the chocolate factory . . .". This factory might well share a common site with a biscuit factory, the latter supplying the basic biscuit to the former for chocolate coating (eg chocolate digestive biscuits).

3. Objective of project

There are various levels of objective. In the above case of the air-conditioning equipment, a general objective would be to prevent chocolate from melting, so that machines and conveyor belts were no longer badly affected by liquid chocolate which would cause stoppages for cleaning, and which would adversely affect the proportion of total chocolate biscuits passing inspection as in a saleable condition. Poor air-conditioning might affect the fresh appearance of such biscuits as well as causing deterioration of surface texture and firmness.

Another kind of objective would involve a clear cut specification along the following lines: (a) to increase the yield of good (chocolate) biscuits from 85 per cent of total (chocolate) biscuits produced to 95 per cent; (b) to reduce machine downtime from one hour per day to fifteen minutes per day, thus increasing gross output from 50,000 biscuits per day to (say) 55,000 biscuits; (c) to reduce inspection costs by 20 per cent; (d) to reduce the level of customer returns from 3 per cent of sales to 1 per cent of sales. A final level of objective would draw (a) to (d) together to measure the return on the capital committed to the project. Many companies have a target figure which must be met in aggregate by all the projects emanating from one source (eg, a particular group location). Thus, the above project might lead to, say, a 35 per cent return on investment (ROI) when the cost of the project, spread over its useful life, plus running costs, was matched against income gains and cost savings through reduced wastage. In many companies, locations requiring heavy expenditure on low performance projects such as safety expenditure, would need to look for consequently higher returns on good projects, say in the cost reduction field so that the aggregate return on all projects was above, say, 35 per cent. Thus local management would be left in no doubt that they had to justify their overall existence in the face of competition from other group locations and from competitors also seeking to justify funding on the money markets.

4. Methods of appraisal used

Inclusion of a comment on the appraisal method used (eg, discounted cash flow, pay-back, etc) is helpful to management because each method has its own particular degree of risk. The degree of risk in using a method of appraisal is caused by approximation, by problems in estimating time scales and precise dates of income and cost incurrence, and sometimes by lack of experience in using particular methods. For example, in ranking a number of competing projects when limited funds were available, one project could appear preferable to the others solely because it offered a very early flow of income. Some methods of appraisal would emphasise this advantage to a particular project, especially when inflation rates, costs of capital, etc were high, while others would place less emphasis on the *timing* of inflows. It might be felt that too much emphasis on timing was inappropriate if timing was based merely on arbitrary guess-work. An alteration to timings by a few months could radically alter the appeal of each project under appraisal.

5. Allowance for time value of money

The rate may be established in advance by the central authority such as a parent company board.

6. Amount and timing of cash flows

Details are particularly important in evaluating risk/degrees of uncertainty. The greater the degree of detail shown, the more comprehensively risk and uncertainty can be measured. Of particular interest is the estimated date when income can first be expected, and how much will be obtained in the earliest periods. Successful start-up of a new project depends on safe arrival of new plant and equipment, etc and on completion of test runs on schedule, and availability of new materials, components etc.

7. Whether all cash items included

Sponsors sending a project forward for final authorisation put their reputations "on the line" at this point. In promoting a local project to, say, a head office in London, it could be unsettling to relationships to omit certain expenses which would emanate from operating the proposed new equipment, such as the air-conditioning plant mentioned above. Head Office staff frequently have the advantage of being able to compare proposed project cash

The Control of Capital Expenditure

flows with those already experienced or planned elsewhere in the group.

8. Accuracy tolerances

Precise costs and income figures take a disproportionately long time to gather. For example, an approximate cost of proposed equipment might be obtainable from a supplier on the telephone (within minutes), whereas the exact order value might not be obtainable for weeks, until the supplier could take precise specifications of his customer's requirement. Again, precise cash inflows might depend on lengthy discussions with sales function's representatives on selling prices, but approximatations could doubtless be agreed much sooner.

9. Methods of continuing control

Those responsible for final authorisation wish to satisfy themselves that actual results are monitored in due course. They need to know whether it will be possible to prove or disprove assertions made under the heading of objectives, eg as regards new yields and downtime. As company cash flow forecasts should be monitored against actual inflows and outflows, so also the same routine comparisons should be employed at project level. The reliability and scope of post-audit procedures are of paramount importance. Strong procedures encourage project sponsors to prepare proposals with great care.

10. Assumptions made

If assumptions are extensive and significant in their potential effect, it may be necessary to prepare a range of possible outcomes in respect of a project, sometimes introducing expressions such as "probable" and "possible". The clearer the list of assumptions, the better the estimate of risk. The total range of assumptions is very similar to that necessary for a company's total cash flow forecast. These assumptions relate to the cost and availability of materials and labour, selling prices of finished products which will be acceptable to the market, tax rates, VAT settlement dates, etc as well as competitor reactions, customer credit worthiness etc.

11. Earlier authorisation levels

In many companies, local management teams are responsible for forwarding potential projects to the central authority (such as the parent company board). Teamwork at local level may be evidenced by a single signature of the senior manager on site, or by the separate signature of each team member. On important projects, once again, reputations are in the balance. In practice certain managers/management teams can, over the years, justify varying degrees of credibility, emanating from blends of experience, business acumen, ranges of vision and conscientiousness in ferreting out possible results of a project.

12. Alternatives considered

There are two tiers to this problem. In the example of the chocolate factory, it would usually be necessary to examine various supplier quotations for air-conditioning equipment and to choose from a range of options. Secondly, where melting chocolate was a serious problem and the reliability of such equipment to do the job for which it was intended was in question, more dramatic options (on a different tier or level) might be considered, such as abandoning that type of product and using building space, plant capacity and the labour force to manufacture an alternative product. Local management would need to remain alert to all possibilities. They would wish to compare the expected outcome of a project with what would happen if it were declined, with projected performance from other projects competing for funds, with ROIs from similar projects in the past, and with the company's overall cut-off point for ROIs.

A diagram can be used to illustrate the range of options which may need consideration:

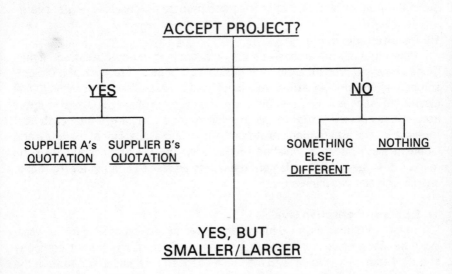

ACCEPT PROJECT?

YES   NO

SUPPLIER A's   SUPPLIER B's   SOMETHING   NOTHING
QUOTATION   QUOTATION   ELSE,
                                      DIFFERENT

YES, BUT
SMALLER/LARGER

Difficulties of attempting post-audit procedures

After a project has been accepted and has been operational for some time, attempts should be made to assess its effectiveness against original estimates. Various factors can make this difficult.

(a) In the case of a replacement investment, the old equipment is often scrapped. Consequently, assertions made by the sponsors of such a project that "the old machinery would have broken down X times per week . . ." can never be proved or disproved.

(b) Many companies do not have accounting systems which are designed to capture actual costs and income analysed by capital project. Thorough comparison of actual and budgeted capital costs and operating results becomes a manual analysis job.

(c) Changing conditions may confuse the issue of whether a project has performed above or below target. A football club might justify the purchase of an expensive striker on the grounds that he would increase the average number of goals scored by the club by one per game, thus raising the club's league position, thus increasing gate money. The actual increase might be two per game, but by the time the striker had taken his place in the team, it could have found itself in th second rather than the first division. Deciding on whether the investment was good would be somewhat confusing.

(d) A company might take the opportunity afforded by a project (and the upheaval caused) to make some non-project alterations. The greatest care would be needed to distinguish project and non-project actual cost during appraisal of purchase invoices, timesheets, stores requisitions, etc.

Conclusion

The evaluation of capital expenditure should be the responsibility of the management of all business functions, who should share opinions and support each other in the use of teamwork. Far more than perfunctory attention should be paid to those within an organisation who have had past experience of the introduction of capital projects.

Chapter 15

THE MEANING OF PRODUCTIVITY AND ITS IMPORTANCE

The value of high productivity

In recent decades, *productivity* has lagged behind profitability among business topics. The former still retains something of its "cloth cap" image, but it is rapidly closing the gap on its over rated stable-mate. Why is productivity now so important?

(1) Its *raison d'etre* is the exploitation of *expensive* resources to maximum advantage — in particular man hours, machine hours, machinery, tooling and materials, rather than money. A major challenge facing industry is to tease more saleable output from each unit of input, be it a bushel of malt, a ton of coal or a machine hour.

(2) Next, productivity contributes to optimising the use of *scarce* resources, such as oil and copper. A company may surmount the crisis of expensive input to production, but there are an ever increasing number of occasions when it cannot find enough for all its needs. In such cases, the company which can utilise what it has in the most economic and *productive* way has a head and shoulders start over competitors.

(3) Productivity yardsticks act as a major and increasingly important supplement to profitability measurements. The latter have (and still do) let through unnoticed inefficiencies, wastage, slow working and poor techniques, provided customers can be found who are willing to "pick up the tab".

(4) Productivity can soak up some of the omnipresent salary and wage awards with which the UK is liberally doused each year, so that they need not be passed on to customers. The benefits of productivity become increasingly obvious, the more such awards fly in the face of a buyer's market in which overseas customers can shop around before deciding where to make purchases.

(5) When sales are the limiting factor, (*ie* when there are too few sales orders to go round), suppliers who have been imbued with the need for high productivity will be most likely to attract custom, being able to under-price rivals and offer improved delivery dates. In the years when high productivity did not particularly matter, some companies nevertheless harvested experience: thus they have optimised their competitiveness.

(6) When there is under-utilisation of total available capacity in the industry concerned, high *productivity* at a particular location within a group predisposes those in authority to favour it with work. Comparative *profitability* or contributions to profit, analysed by group location, used to be paramount. However there has recently been a somersault and comparative productivity has become authenticated as a main criterion for the distribution of scarce orders.

Productivity measurement

Productivity measurement *ratios* are developed by: measuring output, quantifying input of resources used in achieving this output, and then dividing the latter into the former: $\dfrac{\text{OUTPUT}}{\text{INPUT}}$

The result obtained should be compared on·a trend basis with previously set targets, earlier periods and other departments, locations or companies in the same field(s). The fact that a good or bad productivity trend is developing can be grasped so that action may be taken. The precise extent of the trend should not become a focus for.attention. Precise figures provide an aura of credibility which is usually unjustified. Firstly, there may be difficulties in measuring the basic data precisely and/or it is vital to ferret out any distortions which could damage these ratio yardsticks as decision-provoking aids.

Relating to a tiler, for example, the productivity measure $\dfrac{\text{TILES LAID}}{\text{HOURS}}$ developed each month for several months, takes no account of changing tile sizes or qualities month by month on the numerator line. Again, changes in the number of tiles broken are not taken into account. The denominator takes no account of variations in travelling and setting up time, as "hours" presumably would encompass chargeable travelling time which might vary significantly from month to month. In a particular month, a trainee might be used who could ostensibly weaken the productivity performance of that particular period despite being an excellent performer in his own employee category.

The best way to determine the *causes* of a productivity ratio is to break it open; sub-ratios frequently provide the key. For example, a factory's performance of, say, 108 tons of output per man year could be analysed as follows:

$$\text{(A)} \quad \frac{\text{Total tonnage per annum}}{\text{Total number of man years}}$$

$$= \text{(B)} \quad \frac{\text{Total tonnage per annum}}{\text{Value of direct production equipment (£)}} \quad \times \quad \text{(C)} \quad \frac{\text{Value of direct production equipment (£)}}{\text{Total number of man years}}$$

Ratio (B), explored on a trend basis, would show improvements or decline in the weight of output produced per £ of capital equipment. The effects of improving technology and levels of operating skill would be shown subject to the usual concern about possible distortion to the denominator line through provisions for depreciation, revaluations and inflationary increases in equipment costs.

Ratio (C) could reveal the degree of automation prevalent, showing the value of equipment available per man year. The numerator line would need to be treated with care for the reasons mentioned concerning (B).

Again, the analysis could show:

$$\text{(A)} \quad \frac{\text{Total tonnage per annum}}{\text{Total number of man years}}$$

$$= \text{(D)} \quad \frac{\text{Total tonnage per annum}}{\text{Total direct hours worked}} \quad \times \quad \text{(E)} \quad \frac{\text{Total direct hours worked}}{\text{Total number of man years}}$$

Ratio (D) would reveal the output achieved per *direct* hour, without the distortions caused by downtime, waiting time, etc.

Ratio (E) would indicate the number of hours per year which an operator was spending on directly chargeable production. Management would watch for any incipient increase in non-productive paid time per man year, which would cause a decline in the percentage of direct hours within total paid hours.

In cases where accounting expertise is lacking in an organisation, non-monetary productivity ratios can be used to good effect, if circumstances permit. For example, a distibution and warehousing company could consider using

$\dfrac{\text{Number of orders shipped}}{\text{Number of order received}}$ as an indication of whether a backlog of work was building up. A trend could be developed period by period *provided* there was a reasonably constant mix of order types over a number of periods. Clearly, precise trend statistics would be unreliable, as there would be some periods which had a higher or lower proportion of "difficult" orders, but the main objective would not be precision but rather a clear indication of whether a trend was developing, and if so, in what direction. The above approach to productivity measurement, with small means, can be a standing reproach to the elaborate and costly measurement systems which are often found working elsewhere to less effect.

Each organisation which uses productivity ratios should test them against a range of potential uses, to ensure that the time and effort used in their preparation are worthwhile.

For example, a jam factory could consider each of the following ratios:

(1) $\dfrac{\text{LITRES OF JAM}}{\text{MAN YEARS}}$ (2) $\dfrac{\text{TONNES OF FRUIT PULP}}{\text{TONNES OF SUGAR}}$ (3) $\dfrac{\text{LITRES OF JAM}}{\text{OPERATING HOURS}}$

The ensuing table shows how each could be tested:

TEST OF USEFULNESS	$\dfrac{\text{LITRES OF JAM}}{\text{MAN YEARS}}$	$\dfrac{\text{TONNES OF FRUIT PULP}}{\text{TONNES OF SUGAR}}$	$\dfrac{\text{LITRES OF JAM}}{\text{OPERATING HOURS}}$
1. As a reliable basis for wage agreements?			
2. As a test of the benefits of automation?			
3. To test the effects of a shorter working week?			
4. To detect the outcome of a shift from direct to indirect hours of operators?			
5. As a basis for inter-locational competition?			
6. To help to counter inflation?			
7. Is this ratio easy to analyse further?			

Conclusions

Profitability has of course led the ranks of objectives for many years: but a new age has dawned, in which *profitability* without *productivity* is becoming a tinselly illusion. It is possible that in the quest for profitability those at the forefront of trade and commerce, and their financial advisers, may have led sectors of UK industry into a trap. Now that world markets have hardened more than ever, those who have laid the stress on productivity are bound to win.

The time-honoured $\dfrac{\text{Sales £}}{\text{Cost of Sales}}$ yardstick, particularised according to circumstances, as for example $\dfrac{\text{Sales £}}{\text{Labour Cost}}$ or $\dfrac{\text{Sales £}}{\text{Hour}}$ has worn thin. Only those who have also used productivity ratios as self-disciplining and self-assessment techniques are achieving sales in the first place.

The industrialist who knows that his sales invoices are loaded with the cost of slow work, poor tooling, obsolete techniques, etc., but who still has faithful customers and therefore sees no cause for concern because profitability is high, is living on borrowed time.

Chapter 16

THE ROLES OF THE MANAGEMENT ACCOUNTANT

To complete this text, mention should be made of the roles of management accountancy, and those of industrial management accountants.

In defining these roles there is a series of imponderables which, within each organisation's environment, ought to be resolved through a process of teamwork including all managers to whom the management accountant is expected to offer help.

(1) Output reports

(a) There should be explanation of the accuracy tolerances placed on information reports which are prepared. The greater the degree of accuracy demanded, the more expensive in time and effort a report will become.

(b) The assumptions allowed by management in preparing a report should be explained. For example, a wide range of assumptions may initially be included in a costing report showing the comparative costs of choosing from several courses of action. Some of these assumptions may be unacceptable: unless they are exposed for discussion, wrong decisions may be made.

(c) Timing tolerances should be agreed: as with production scheduling, the management accountant should, with the help of colleagues, produce information reports in good time, but if he is required to produce them too early, he may need to employ extra staff, and/or the quality of the data rushed into a reporting system to make the reports possible may be suspect.

(2) Materiality of costs

In a nutshell, the management accountant should not spend disproportionate amounts of time on trivial elements of cost; nor should his reports encourage others to do so.

(3) Responsibilities

The management accountant's colleagues have significant parts to play in, for example, defining precisely their own information reporting needs, preparing budgets and addressing the questions raised by variances from plans. "Who does what" must be explained and continually re-assessed.

(4) Split objectives

The management accountant must frequently serve local site management and also the head of his own function at an organisation's headquarters. He must ensure that the requests for aid to be given to one are not in contention with those for the other.

The management accountant's specific roles
(1) The specialist

The inherent danger to an individual management accountant lies in a narrowing of his experience and training. While qualified staff nowadays are hired by far-sighted organisations only if they appear to have career development potential, extensive specialisation over long periods impedes mobility to other areas of responsibility within the function or indeed to other functions or to general management. At the same time, however, the complex nature of the role which the accountancy function must play demands high levels of expertise in those who have a part to play, and this can be achieved over a period of time by those who specialise.

Thus we have the interests of the individual apparently in conflict with those of the function as a whole. However, looking more closely, can it be safely assumed that, in the long term, a set of specialists are desirable to the accountancy function of a particular organisation? If specialists leave, or retire, and there is no-one within the organisation to replace them except specialists from other fields, recruitment has to take place from outside.

There is no easy answer to this situation. One step which can be taken is to train each specialist to a keen appreciation of the responsibilities, problems and objectives of the other specialists within the function. In this way promotion of a specialist within the function becomes logical. However the key persons should move around within the function if it is a large one, so that when the time comes for a more general management position, they can call on first-hand experience. This policy of course means that everyone engaged temporarily or permanently in specialist work must respond to the challenge of training others, being only stewards of the sections in which they work. This can be facilitated by ensuring that there is adequate documentation of procedures, manuals of instructions to staff, clearly defined objectives for each area, and comprehensive job specifications for all concerned.

(2) The fire-fighter

Fire-fighting is necessary when the resources (including information), deployed by an organisation in attempting to meet specific objectives fail to do so. The re-deployment of resources is involved including man-power and, in the present context, the management accountant's time. Frequently the management accountant will find himself performing in areas which are not in his job specification. The elimination of the need for fire-fighting is very difficult, but it can be aided by a comprehensive approach to planning and the anticipation of possible problem areas. After all, fire-fighting generally takes place when something unexpected happens for which there has been insufficient preparation.

(3) The fact-finder

The management accountant is often bombarded with requests for information by all and sundry, mainly because of his unique position of having access to written records. These ad hoc requests are often not anticipated, and in such cases can contribute to the pressure which is a common characteristic of accountancy. Ad hoc requests for information tend also to direct the accountant from the work shown in his job specification and also from his objectives.

In ensuring that special fact-finding exercises are worthwhile, the management accountant needs to turn to top management for a lead, as they set objectives which should result in harmony of effort across functional frontiers. If everyone works towards those objectives then ad hoc requests from other functions should cause less consternation to the accountancy function. Sudden requests for information are to be expected, but the degree of anticipation which the accountant has exercised dictates the level of upheaval which results.

Conclusion
(a)   The role of management accountancy

This is directed essentially from Board level and centres on the provision of management information necessary to enable the organisation to achieve its objectives. The Board gives direction to the efforts of the rest of the organisation. Its separate instructions to each of the various business functions must achieve a general harmony of such efforts. Management information provided by the accountancy function facilitates rapid movement in the direction laid down by the Board and is consequently designed to promote decision making. To achieve this, the information must be timely, accurate and meaningful.

(b)   The role of individual accountants

The goal for the accountancy function must be to determine the particular sets of circumstances and conditions which will optimise individual contributions towards the fulfilment of the accountancy function's objectives. In other words, everyone must take up a team position. In football not everyone can be centre-forward, and if more than one man tries to be goal-keeper, penalties are incurred which seriously undermine the team's chance of winning. The key to success is that each player operates in a role suited to his particular skills and training.

Further Useful Reading

An Engineers Guide to Costing published by the Institute·of Cost & Management Accountants in conjunction with the Institution of Production Engineers. *Understanding Management Acounting* by the same author, published by Gee & Co (Publishers) Ltd, 151 Strand, London WC2R 1JJ.

INDEX

NOTES

NOTES

NOTES